The Experience of Songs

THE EXPERIENCE OF SONGS

MARK W. BOOTH

NEW HAVEN AND LONDON
YALE UNIVERSITY PRESS

Published with the assistance of the
Frederick W. Hilles Publication Fund.

Designed by James J. Johnson
and set in Linotron Bodoni type.
Printed in the United States of America by
The Alpine Press, Stoughton, Mass.

Library of Congress Cataloging in Publication Data

Booth, Mark W., 1943–
    The experience of songs.

    Includes index.
    1. Songs, English—History and criticism.
2. Songs, American—History and criticism.
I. Title.
PR507.B63   821'.04'09   81–972
ISBN 0–300–02622–6

10 9 8 7 6 5 4 3 2 1

To Robert Norman Booth

Contents

Acknowledgments

I owe special thanks for the aid and encouragement of Edward Doughtie and of Michael Paull. I am grateful for the help given me by Polly Berends, Boyd Berry, Elizabeth Berry, Edwin Black, Joseph Bogen, Gordon Bok, Cleta Booth, Elisabeth Brocking, E. Allan Brown, David Buchan, Keith Crim, Walter Dubler, Bernie Einbond, A. B. Friedman, Christine Gallant, James Gallant, Susan Gohlman, Ellen Graham, Marguerite Harkness, John Heptonstall, Sonia Heptonstall, Joseph Hickerson, Tom Inge, Barry Katz, Gordon Kelly, Jim Kinney, Stanley Lindberg, Kurt Link, Norton Lockard, Bob McNutt, Mike Miller, Mary Frances Minton, Charlotte Morse, Joan Muller, Fred Nichols, Ivan Perry, R. G. Peterson, Alejandro Planchart, Richard Priebe, Victor Reed, Stan Rubin, William Sisler, Lucy Stretch, Ron Bean Tobias, Mary Anne Turner, Craig Williamson, Elizabeth Williamson, and Susan Woolford.

A portion of the book was written during the period of a grant from the Grants-in-Aid Program for Faculty of Virginia Commonwealth University. I wish to thank the Advisory Committee of that program and its chairman, John J. Salley. Portions of this work have appeared in slightly different form in *The Quarterly Journal of Speech* 62, *The Georgia Review* 32, no. 2 (essay entitled "Ballad and the Brain"), and *The Chaucer Review* 14, no. 2. I wish to thank the editors of these journals for permission to include this previously published material.

Introduction:
Words in Songs

HEN THE STAGE clears at the end of *Twelfth Night*, the clown Feste remains behind to sing a song. This is what he sings:

When that I was and a little tine boy,
*   with hey, ho, the winde and the raine:*
A foolish thing was but a toy,
*   for the raine it raineth every day.*

But when I came to mans estate,
*   with hey ho, the winde and the raine:*
Gainst Knaves and Theeves men shut their gate,
*   for the raine it raineth every day.*

But when I came alas to wive,
*   with hey ho, the winde and the raine:*
By swaggering could I never thrive,
*   for the raine it raineth every day.*

But when I came unto my beds,
*   with hey ho, the winde and the raine:*
With tospottes still had drunken heades,
*   for the raine it raineth every day.*

A great while ago the world begon,
*   hey ho, the winde and the raine:*
But that's all one, our Play is done,
*   and wee'l strive to please you every day.*

The song has a curious critical history. Shakespeare's early editors and commentators were notably unimpressed with it. In the eighteenth century Warburton wrote, "This wretched stuff not *Shakespeare's*, but the Players!" Capell agreed: "Either this song was one then in vogue . . . or else, the composition of the Clown, and so lug'd into the play without rime or reason; or if indeed Shakespeare's . . . a thing idly drop'd from him upon some other occasion." Steevens found it "scarce credible, that after he had cleared his stage, he should exhibit his Clown afresh, and with so poor a recommendation as this song. . . . [a] nonsensical ditty . . . some buffoon actor's composition."[1]

Later scholars were more willing, and even determined, to find merit in the song. Charles Knight first praised it a century and a half ago as "philosophical wisdom . . . a treatise might be written upon its wisdom." In the 1920s Richmond Noble called it "wise nonsense," and the Arden editor found in it "the philosophy of human life." More restrained and more persuasive things have been said by others, but these relatively bold pronouncements provide a useful index to what Shakespeareans have wanted to find when they have read, and helped others read, these lines.

They have wanted above all for the lines to make sense. This standard would seem to be a low one, but for many readers the song has, unfortunately, met it inadequately. Capell wrote: "Whoso wishes to strike a few sparks of reason from it, must . . . turn decypherer; as thus: the pursuits of the speaker, and his disappointments in some of them, in four stages of life, are severally describ'd in as many stanzas."[2] That this much story is enciphered into the words of the text, Capell by no means persuaded himself, inclined as he was to imagine it "idly drop'd" by its author. The sense he hoped to find was narrative, and it is easy to see why he concluded in exasperation that the story was at best carelessly told. A modern critic, Leslie Hotson, decodes the story with a different key—"indecency."

> Nature was commonly believed to have endowed the Fool with an excess of virility, symbolized by his *bauble.* . . . *Thing* in

its "bauble" sense is the key word. . . . In the Fool's childish state as a little tiny boy, a *foolish thing* was no more than a harmless trifle. . . . In the second stanza . . . the lecherous knave finds that his goatish vice renders him an outcast, shut out in the rain.[3]

And so on. Sense, if it were presumed found in this reading, would again be narrative sense, a veiled history.

The defenders who have found not only narrative but also veiled philosophy credit the song with a different kind of sense— discursive sense, which would make a moral for the play. So the Arden editor: "Guilt reaps its own reward. . . . [The song serves] to remind us that we must return to realities, that life is a serious business, and that 'it is not good to stay too long in the Theater' (Bacon, *Advancement of Learning*)."[4] Finally, John Hollander has seen

a summation of the play in many ways at once . . . a kind of quick rehearsal of the Ages of Man. . . . Lechery, trickery, dissembling and drunkenness, inevitable and desperate in mundane existence . . . are just those activities which, min-gled together in a world of feasting, serve to purge man of the desire for them.[5]

This last is searching commentary on *Twelfth Night*, but it may be doubted whether the song makes any such commentary. The quest for sense has dug below the song, has broken through, and is min-ing the text of the play.

Peter Seng, whose edition of Shakespeare's songs assembles these and many other comments on this song, concludes with wise caution that beyond minimum obvious meaning and function, "whatever else it may be would best be left to viewers of the play. No one who has ever heard it sung to Vernon's music would wish it omitted." The appeal to performance is a good idea, and the testi-mony from that appeal carries weight, despite its subjectivity. Whether or not it is strictly true that no one ever wished the song dropped, the claim raises the main issue. Perhaps the song is worthless; but if it is any good at all and yet makes as little narrative or discursive sense as so far seems to be the case, what good is it? What good is in it? As edited text, it has yielded but little to the demands of reading scholars. Their questions have not been very fruitful. What are some alternative questions, in response to which we may hope it will unfold more fully? What are the right questions to ask about a song?

This book is an attempt to identify such questions and to experiment with the asking of them. Let us begin by describing the challenge posed by this song:

1. It does not make much sense, and it does not say a great deal. That is, it is short on narrative content and obscure as to a possible moral. What other kinds of sense might a song make; what else might a song be good at besides saying things?

2. Whether or not it was assembled by Shakespeare, much of it is not Shakespearean. Half of the lines are repetitive refrain, more or less the refrains of various popular songs of the time. Part of the rest is highly conventional, like the standard "wive-thrive" rhyme, which determines the sentiment of those lines to be likewise conventional. What merit can it have if it is put together from proverbs and conventional tags?

3. The phrasing that does seem attributable to Shakespeare is casual and approximate, "a very loose syntax . . . to ensure perfect conformation to the tune pattern," as one critic observes, although regrettably we are not sure of the tune.[6] What is the art of a lyric that disdains elegance of language?

4. Despite the labor spent to bring the song around to telling an elliptical story, we might even suspect that it is not necessarily completely ordered, or even complete; or, on the other hand, it might even do without some of what we have of it. The effect of the song would undoubtedly be the same if the clown were to forget one of the middle stanzas; it would be about the same if he rearranged them. The stanzas of Shakespeare's song "It was a Lover and his lasse" in *As You Like It* have been rearranged from their Folio order by modern editors; probably they were jumbled there

in the first place because in some or all early performances only the first and last stanzas were sung. How can song suffer these violations and have integrity, wholeness, beauty?

These obstacles seem to be enough to doom appreciative analysis of the form and content of these lines of song verse. Yet these clownishly clumsy, unpretentiously conventional verses participate in a distinctive, appropriate, beautiful whole song. Further, when they are understood as words for music, they can be more soundly and fully understood than they are in the criticism that has been quoted here—and this even though we do not know with certainty what that music was, how it spaced, phrased, emphasized, or decorated the verses. Even if we only postulate music with these words, we can hear them better. To see how this may be so, we must now consider some aspects of the nature of songs.

Defining song is a descriptive and exploratory matter. When measured language is carried through a tune, it has been sung, and it is probably but not necessarily song. A song consists of, for one thing, a not-very-long stretch of music, which may or may not be strophically repeated but which does have a distinct closure after it sets a moderate number of lines of verse; and for the other, a certain quantity of song verse. The verse of song is the primary interest of the present study. Song verse is a broad domain that has generally been lightly regarded and badly understood, and, although certain borders may be ragged, this domain is a unified whole.

Outside the borders and not bound to share the nature of song are words merely recited to music and words sung in recitative or in liturgical or other chant. More difficult to map is the important area where song verse and lyric poetry that is not song meet. Any poetical text can of course be yoked by violence to music, but much poetry cannot thereby be transformed into song. This distinction is commonly made, quite rightly, on the ground that poetry is often too complicated or dense to be done justice in singing. Paul Valéry said that hearing poetry set to music is like seeing a painting through a stained-glass window. This judgment of course presumes "poetry" to mean some verse and not other verse; and the distinction is not simply between good and bad verse. The distinction, to be satisfactory, must separate Shakespeare's songs from his sonnets, and the singing from the nonsinging verse of Wyatt, Sidney, Dryden, Burns, Tennyson, and other writers, as well as songs of all species from both good and bad lyric poetry.

Although this valuable distinction is difficult to make precise, it can be made plain. The more familiar claims are those of "poetry," but there is an alternative mode in which verse may exist, with laws to itself: that of song verse. To establish that this alternative exists, it is useful to see that it is made up of subordinate provinces which, from the common point of view in the realm of "poetry," are apt to be seen as separate outlying appendages of that realm rather than as belonging together, united by a common nature. To see that these phenomena thought of as separate are parts of another whole is to understand better not only song but also poetry. Folk ballad, sophisticated stage song, and pop hit are usually taken to be at least as firmly partitioned from each other as any is from poetry. The best texts of any may be allowed over into an anthology of poems under the prevailing assumption that the single distinction to be made is whether it reads well there. This, to use the geopolitical metaphor for the last time, is a sort of imperialism. Where the song properly exists, where it is words for the singing voice, it has possibilities not recognized among poems for reading. It shares that unapprehended potential with the texts taken in from apparently widely different directions. Their kinship is, I think, much greater than is usually assumed. Song in its diversity is also one thing.

The succeeding chapters will return repeatedly to consider what it means to take certain verses for song and to distinguish them from poetry that is not song. The basis for this distinction must be sought in consideration of the central tendencies of song and examination of the forms and functions broadly characteristic of the scattered kinds of song verse.

SONG AS ORAL COMMUNICATION

The existence of songs in sound, in time, is the simplest distinction between them and written verse. Song words are given only once in a performance and then are gone, carried along by the music and succeeded implacably by the next words, which claim attention in their turn. Even if one sings alone, to please oneself, one is reluctant to hesitate, grope, and correct one's words. If the reader of printed words says to a phrase, "Oh, stay, thou art so fair" (or so obscure), it will stay. If his mind has slackened attention and missed something, he can look back and find it. Words only heard are not forgiving in this way. Song words bear the burden of oral communication, under the special condition of being set to music.

Song words need not themselves be particularly musical in sound. Verse that is very highly patterned with musical sound of its own may clash with the music of its tune. Except in pursuit of certain special effects, as in lullabies, verse does not qualify for song by approaching the condition of music. Song verse is not assimilated to music but accommodated to it. Words must be adapted to assertive regulation by the tones and rhythm of music upon their own sound and pace. Music dictates that certain qualities of the individual words, and of the patterns into which they fall, are appropriate for song while others are not. W. H. Auden argues that a certain quality of boldness is needed in the words: those best suited for song are "those which require the least reflection to comprehend . . . most dynamic and immediate . . . interjections . . . imperatives; verbs of physical action . . . or physical concomitants of emotion." Bertrand Bronson shows how, in the traditional ballads, music governs what words can do: "Units of thought are made commensurate with the four-stress musical phrase . . . structure and meaning must be immediately seized by the ear." He sees the music requiring "simple confrontations of agreement and disagreement" and discouraging subtlety or irony.[7]

The ways in which song words are subject to the pressure of

their music are subtle and fascinating. They are reinforced, accented, blurred, belied, inspired to new meaning, in a continual interplay. In that interplay there is a constant tug against the resolution of the words to carry out their own business. The words must have an internal discipline to maintain their integrity in their cooperation and in their competition with the music. They must contend with the positive distraction threatened by the accompaniment, and the fact of this threat of distraction opens a way into analysis of the general forms such words take.

Song verse shares some of the characteristics of true oral poetry—and also differs from it in important ways. Song belongs to both nonliterate and literate cultures, having originated in the former and been naturalized in the latter. In a literate age songs are written down before they come to an audience. They are a species of script. Although some song is composed today without writing, most is composed with its help; and even when no writing is directly involved, our songs are made by people who *can* write, a crucial distinction from "primary" orality. The subject will be examined closely in discussion of oral ballad in chapter 3.

The study of oral epic begun by Milman Parry and continued by Albert B. Lord showed that illiterate oral poets in modern Europe, and by forceful inference also in Homer's time, were craftsmen in an art whose essence is the extemporaneous manipulation of formulas. A "singer of tales" chants his epic anew, unique at each performance, by drawing on a repertoire of formulas of epithet, phrase, line, and plot contour.[8] Lord's study stresses the use of formulas as the necessary recourse of the artist who has to keep going, to keep coming up with the next lines of his narrative. For our purposes we may consider that this mode of operating not only eases the burden on the poet but also accommodates the audience of oral poetry, which to some extent is always hearing something it knows and hence is able to keep up despite distractions and the essentially volatile nature of attention itself. Listeners hear and recognize phrases and lines, and the new whole is built from these recognized elements. The formulas that are part of the repertoire of the oral poet are also part of the repertoire of the au-

dience. Neither repertoire is clearly definable—no one could re-
cite in series all the phrases he knows—nor are the formulas
perfectly rigid: variation of the formulas is as much the art of the
poet as is linking them together. But the units have a high degree
of familiarity to their proper audience.

An important consequence of this fact is that the units cannot,
in themselves, say very much to the audience. E. H. Gombrich,
discussing the codes needed when communication takes place,
says of the units in such codes that "the greater the probability of
a symbol's occurrence in any given situation, the smaller will be
its information content. Where we can anticipate we need not listen."[9] The communications theorist Norbert Wiener applies this
fact specifically to the present issue: "It is possible to interpret
the information carried by a message as essentially the negative
of its entropy, and the negative logarithm of its probability. That
is, the more probable the message, the less information it gives.
Clichés, for example, are less illuminating than great poems."[10]
Oral poetry has a relatively lower density of information per line
than written poetry can have. The units are more familiar; or,
to put it another way, they are larger: the audience recognizes
phrases more often and is less often cued by the subtle surprises
of individual words.

This low density of information characteristic of oral poetry
(chanted, but not sung to melody) shows also in song verse, when
it is set beside verse written for the page. Only excessively trite
songs, though such songs certainly exist, are thoroughly formulaic, being built entirely of spare parts of other songs. (Oral
poetry is not absolutely formulaic either.) If instead of prefabrica-
tion, however, we speak of a degree of redundancy, of predictabil-
ity, varying from full surprise to full certainty, then a good deal of
redundancy is characteristic of the words of songs—more than in
most written communication and much more than is usual in written poetry.[11]

Such redundancy in song is achieved by a variety of means.
One, the most like formula, is the simple borrowing of a line from
another well-known song, or even the sharing of it in a family of

songs, as with the formulas in traditional ballads. "It was in and
about the Martinmas time" serves for the first line of some versions of the melancholy ballad of "Bonny Barbara Allen," and "It
fell about the Martinmas time" is used as the first line of the jocular "Get Up and Bar the Door." Both the somber "Douglas Tragedy" and the flippant "Baffled Knight" may use the line "He's
mounted her on a milk-white steed." [12] It is important and perhaps
surprising that a borrowing in song seldom refers attention to any
source, except so far as casual allusion may build up mood or
tone. An American labor song from the thirties begins "I dreamed
I saw Joe Hill last night / Alive as you and me"; the opening was
used thirty years later by Bob Dylan as "I dreamed I saw St. Au-
gustine / Alive as you or me." [13] The two songs have little in common beyond these lines, though much of the audience for the second probably had heard the first. There seems to be little allusive
value to the borrowing. The replication of the second line, given
the replication of the first, seems to follow mainly because two
lines is the size of this unit.

Borrowings come from other sources than songs in the experience of the song's public: from proverbs, dicta, slang, from the
jargon of preachers, politicians, advertisers, sportscasters. Medieval carols often used proverbial phrases for their burdens:

An old sawe hath be fownd trewe:
"Cast not away thyn old for newe." [14]

Popular song writers of the present have done the same:

You don't tug on Superman's cape
You don't spit into the wind
You don't pull the mask off the old Lone Ranger
And you don't mess around with Jim. [15]

The artistry of popular song sometimes consists in the juxtaposition of formulas from subtly different realms of public talk:

It's anybody's ballgame
It's everybody's fight. . . . [16]

Redundancy is achieved in a borrowing when the line is known to the specific audience of the song. It is not easy to say what specific audiences are, but it is important to know that songs have them. In a complex and differentiated society it is not the nature of most songs to be open to the general public. In popular music in this country today the habitual phrases of soul singers are recognizable to one audience, those of country-western to another, those of glossy pop to another. That styles of song have distinct audiences is the commonsense presumption of marketing in the modern music industry. The proprietary relationship of such audiences to their styles is largely a matter of culturally conditioned musical preferences, but it depends also on, or is significantly reinforced by, the patterns of words that are set to the music. Audiences are ready for their songs to say certain things in certain ways.

There are other means to redundancy besides borrowing. Artful song words call on various devices to prepare their reception. One of these is internal repetition, the leading structural principle of many styles of song, especially those that spring from or mimic improvisation—dance song, work song, blues.

Polly put the kettle on
Polly put the kettle on
Polly put the kettle on
We'll all have tea.[17]

I ain't never loved but three womens in my life
I ain't never loved but three womens in my life
My mother and my sister and my partner's wife.[18]

The technique lends itself to many effects, but one function is simply getting the first proposition firmly fixed with an audience or a group of participants. Many other species of song quote themselves from one stanza to another, as in the incremental repetition of the English traditional ballads, in choruses, or in the return to the opening stanza for conclusion, which seems natural in a very wide variety of lyrics.

The formal constraints of verse in general serve song verse in this pursuit of partial redundancy. Rhyme and meter increase it, and song relies heavily on emphatic meter and on rhyming, often dense short-range rhyming that looks Skeltonic on paper:

You say yes
I say no
You say stop
And I say go, go, go
Oh, no
You say goodbye
And I say hello
Hello hello
I don't know why
You say goodbye
I say hello.[19]

Antithesis, both within lines and between succeeding lines and stanzas, is also extremely common, one pole preparing for the other, as in the "simple confrontations of agreement and disagreement" in the ballad. Various natural pairings and groupings serve the same way: past and present, present and future; sun and rain; sunrise, sunset; birds and bees; a fish in the water, a bird in the air.

Now well and nowe woo
Now frend and nowe foo
  Thus goth this worlde iwys . . .[20]

Alliteration is endemic in song lines; it is sometimes a pleasant sound in itself, but it also contributes to redundancy.

The clubs are all closed
And the ladies are leavin'
There's nobody nobody knows on the street
A few stranded souls
Standin' cold at the station
With nowhere to go but to bed and to sleep.[21]

A special case of structural redundancy is described by Edward Doughtie in an analysis of Elizabethan song:

> The songs are full of . . . rhetorical devices. . . . Any educated person would have been familiar with most of these tropes and figures from school, and would take pleasure in hearing them well used. . . . Rhetoric also had the advantage of ordering language in such a way that the hearer, recognizing the form, would more easily assimilate the content since it would be partly expected. [22]

Finally, this catalogue of devices includes the punning and double entendre favored by some styles of song, in which cases a word has two justifications because it makes two kinds of sense and hence has a higher probability, a sum of two probabilities. A punning word, that is, has two reasons to be where it is, and though it is a surprise when met, it is especially the right word once we recognize the pun, right in two ways at once.

I've got the lemon and the
Chicken cordon bleus.[23]

I haue a gentil cook   [cock]
   crowyt me day . . .
and euery nyʒt he perchit hym
   in myn ladyis chaumbyr.[24]

However the redundancy is built up, the song typically gives its audience a wealth of cues to help it catch a line.

Given the relationship of redundancy to information, a songwriter should not have anything really new to say, at least if he expects to say it with the words of the song alone. A poet on paper has much greater freedom to test the patience and ingenuity of the reader and to stretch his comprehension. He can aspire to enlarge the reader's world of experience and ideas. But a song, hedged by the demands of unity and clarity, must say things that are simplifications, and generally familiar simplifications. The experience of a new song must be the imagining anew of some simplification of life that is more or less in our possession already. It does not follow that what is said, well or badly, by the words of songs is unimportant. It can be profoundly important. We can understand the nature of the things songs say by inquiring into the nature of the response that song awakens in a listener.

THE POINT OF VIEW OF SONG

To appreciate how an audience experiences what a song says, consider the element of vocal performance of song, apprehended either immediately or through some electronic mediation. Song words are delivered to us by someone's voice (or by our own, the case to which, as will appear in a moment, other cases converge). The voice of another person who is not, like an actor in a play would be, addressing his voice overtly to some other specific person, a voice without dramatic context, presents itself as a medium of communication from someone else to me. As the flat eyes in a painting or the finger of Uncle Sam point at the observer, undirected spoken words direct themselves straight toward any listener. One may read with equanimity a sign saying "Exit" or even "Abandon all hope, ye who enter here." But when the stooge on television delivers a commercial message, I surrender an involuntary smile of social agreeableness; when the recording at the Los Angeles airport admonishes against parking, it is very difficult to proceed to park. Words from a voice are privileged in their power to arrest attention. We appoint ourselves the addressees.

We have the same impulse with sung words, attending to them as if they were spoken, and spoken to us in particular. Of course that impulse is in tension with our whole perception of the song as art—it rhymes, it fits the music—and only the specially naive may think "this song is just for me." As a listener I participate in the communication, or pseudocommunication, of the voice only in an anonymous way, as a member of the group that is the audience of any given song. So the song is not mistaken directly for a message to me, although it plays on my tendency to take it that way. It is a performance for me-and-fellows. The singer sings, we generally say, *for* his audience. The performance is, in the first place, for its audience in the sense that it is going on in front of listeners as an object of their attention.

But the experience of song for the members of its proper audience makes them more than listeners. Because song comes to us in a voice, without dramatic context, to pass through the consciousness of the listener, it fosters some degree of identification between singer and audience. The soprano Lotte Lehmann wrote that the singer works "without the footlights which separate so wonderfully the world of the stage from the world of reality. You stand close to the audience. Almost one with it, you take it, so to speak, by the hand and say: 'Let us live this song together!'"[25] Whether or not it always happened just like this when Miss Lehmann sang German lieder for Americans, her ideal description is beautifully apt for all kinds of songs. When this ideal is achieved, when this fusion is entered into by the listeners, the performance is *for* the audience in a second sense: the singer's words are sung for us in that he says something that is also said somehow in extension *by* us, and we are drawn into the state, the pose, the attitude, the self offered by the song. This is to some extent the description of the other performing arts as well, though not so distinctively as of song; further, it is the description of ritual. The individual member of the audience enters into a common pattern of thought, attitude, emotion, and achieves by it concert with his society. When we hear song, we are the concert. A rock concert, for example, may be described as ritual, in which representative figures sing out fantasies for and also with the audience. It seems to me that such a description can be applied very widely to the experience of many varieties of song. C. M. Bowra writes of primitive song that it is "a communal activity . . . to some degree the voice of a common consciousness." He goes on to say, "This is of course true of modern singing, especially when it is done for pleasure," although he believes that "primitive song implies a higher degree of shared assumptions."[26]

Speaking on behalf of the audience is an effect felt even in narrative song, which tells stories for us. If we find the song appealing, we adopt the story, and tell it along with the singer. The story is our testimony. Thus traditional ballads tell stories the audience knows and affirms, and to understand them we must think of them as stories a people tells itself—not in the old romantic sense of the folk composing but in the sense that narrative song implies audience affirmation. The stories attest class values, for example. It is not necessary that narrative have a sense of lesson to it for this feeling of testimony to obtain. The ballads often give highly objective and impersonal accounts of dire or uncanny events—a good example is "The Wife of Usher's Well"[27]—but this very impersonal quality suggests a function through identification: perhaps it is not far from a common understanding of such ballads to say that they serve as proverbs may serve, proverbs likewise being things that we tell ourselves. They say, that is, "Yes, the world is like this, such things happen," and so help to control the fearfulness such kinds of events might inspire.

Notice that in the case of narrative song we do not identify with a character in the song, but with the teller, with his implicit attitudes or his projected state. Tear-jerking narrative song gives us the experience not of the suffering character but of the sympathizing teller. In the old ballad of "Sir Patrick Spens," the listener does not enter into the dismay and then heroic resolution of the hero, or the loneliness of the survivors, but rather into admiration for the hero, joined with contempt for the dandified nobles. In Bob Dylan's ballad of Hollis Brown, the feelings roused in the audience are not those of the despairing farmer, but those of the indignant narrator pointing his accusatory finger.[28] Thus most songs of protest do not appeal to an audience as jury but invite the already sympathetic into collective accusation; they promote complacency by reinforcement, and are likelier to issue in self-congratulation than in persuasion or action.

In a song where the singer addresses a second person (saying, in all probability, "I love you"), the audience identifies with the speaking voice, and this effect is so compelling as not necessarily to respect even difference of sex: a man who hears a woman sing a declaration of love generally identifies himself, I think, with declarer and not with beloved. This effect is usually true in printed lyric; if it is also true of sung lyric, it is because the identification with a voice is a remarkably strong force, sweeping us past the stage of aesthetic contemplation and even past the fantasy that the words are directed to us. To give a perhaps more persuasive case than love song, Dylan's scornful "Positively 4th Street" that begins "You got a lotta nerve / To say you are my friend" surely has found no guilty listener who identifies with the addressee.[29] Given the dramatic context of a stage, the same words might well draw sympathetic identification toward the figure who takes the abuse; without context, we abuse, the singer abuses for us. Oddly, the more vigorously such songs declare lonely alienation, the better they function as rituals of solidarity in an accepted state of mind.

The mechanism of identification fails if the state offered us is not acceptable: the song may seem repugnant, or, more likely, simply uninteresting. Thus song words do not lend themselves readily to the appreciation of a cultural outsider with anything like the satisfaction they make available to the audience for whom those words affirm something. Our songs always embody snippets of the myths we hold, we the culture or subculture who make the proper audience. By "myth" here is meant myth as giver of identity, as template for self. The song embodies myth and we step into it. The blues singer who voices lonely pain does it for all his listeners and gives them a state to enter, and an attitude toward that state, that is part of the defining myth and self-defining ethic of his and their culture—or of a culture to which one wishes to imagine he belongs. My strong feelings of identification with a favorite singer draw upon associations that are as complicated as my life, and the singer's performance is likewise full of nuance. Yet any number of other listeners are also achieving an identification, and the song is our common denominator.

SONG AS TRANSCENDENCE

A striking analysis of the nature of song was offered by Victor Zuckerkandl as the basis for his study of the meaning of music,

published unfinished after his death in 1965. Zuckerkandl set out
to show that musicality is an aspect of our essential human nature, and that through the experience of music (though not only
through music) we attain "broader, deeper levels of existence."
Music, he contends, "surely provides the shortest, the least ar-
duous, perhaps even the most natural solvent of artificial boundaries between the self and others."[30] He argues that in a practical,
not mystical, way music gives access to a whole dimension of reality added to those dimensions of time and space where we find
ourselves and others and things separate and sequential.

> People sing in order to make sure, through direct experience,
> of their existence in a layer of reality different from the one in
> which they encounter each other and things as speakers, as
> facing one another and separate from one another—in order
> to be aware of their existence on a plane where distinction and
> separation of man and man, man and thing, thing and thing
> give way to unity, to authentic togetherness.[31]

These remarks may not be unfamiliar in their general tenor as
suggesting that the world of musical experience is in some sense
above or apart from mundane reality of space and time. Philosophical formulations on the subject are founded on very common
and unesoteric facts about music: the fact of harmony, for example, where two or more plainly distinct notes exist apart but simultaneous, and the fact of tune, where tones move around somewhere and come back to rest in some invisible place.

What I take to be distinctive in the argument advanced by
Zuckerkandl is his insistence that the place entered into in the
experience of music is specifically a place of unity, of communion
of the subjective self with all else. He bases this argument on an
analysis of song, showing how musical tones transform speech
away from the presupposition of separations among speaker, hear-
er, and object of discourse. So important, in fact, is the distinction he makes between singing and speaking man that the transition he posits from song to other music is abrupt and doubtful. "In
all the foregoing," he says at that transition, "'singing man' stands

for 'music-making man' in the broadest sense: after all, it does not really matter whether one makes music with the natural instrument of the vocal cords or with a man-made instrument. . . . Music-making man is singing man." His discussion of how tones work on words is offered to make explicit changing relationships of subject to objective world that he believes persist when the tones do not accompany words.

Zuckerkandl's discussion specifically of song argues two kinds of "self-abandon . . . where subject and object come together." The first is between persons, the identification urged already in this introduction.

> The words of folk song . . . are not directed by one person to another or by many persons to many others; the voice is that of the group . . . there is no "other being," no mere listeners. . . . If one member of the group happens to lead the chorus, his words are certainly not addressed to the others. . . . He does not tell them anything they don't know; he does not speak to the others but *for* them. [32]

As opposed to speaking, singing of words joins the single self with its community. This effect, he continues, would also be observable if people made only nonverbal music together; but people sing words, and words refer to things. Singing about things is evidence of a second kind of self-transcendence operating in song.

> The singer who uses words wants more than just to be with the group: he also wants to be with things, those things to which the words of the poem refer. . . . [Tones] remove the barrier between person and thing, and clear the way for what might be called the singer's inner participation in that of which he sings. [33]

This part of Zuckerkandl's theory will be illustrated by various examples in discussions later in this book. When we examine a broadside ballad about a monstrous whale, we will see how the song takes on a boastful pride in the whale's amazing proportions.

A sea shanty that describes a certain kind of voyage assimilates the work the men are doing, while singing, to that imagined voyage, and so on.

There is one further stage to this annihilation of distance in song: if we come into real unity with things sung about, those things cannot be separate in that dimension of reality from each other, either: "In the layer of reality whence the tones come and toward which they lead, not only the antithesis of 'I' and 'it' but also the distinctions between things are transcended. There must be a layer in which all things have their roots."[34] Thus follows the eloquent judgment already quoted: "People sing in order to make sure, through direct experience, of their existence . . . where distinction and separation . . . give way to authentic togetherness."

Zuckerkandl's argument, giving as it does a lofty idea of the significance of song in the humanness itself of human experience, is clearly an encouragement to further investigation of the specifics of songs. He locates the power of music in its enabling of self-transcendence for the listener and demonstrates that function in folk song; he attaches fundamental importance for the whole realm of music to the shift of point of view which he detects there. What of the realm of words? Zuckerkandl's study is apparently less encouraging for investigation into the words that are sung to music. What happens when a singer is lifted out of selfhood, he claims, is indicated by words but explained by, or referred to, music, and it is finally independent of bodily voices and of any words they might carry. Words in song testify, he says, only to what music is doing on its own. At worst the implication might be that what words in what patterns go with music is strictly irrelevant, since everything that rises into the musical dimension must converge.

We have seen that the things song words say, since they can not be too idiosyncratic or complex in diction, images, and themes, tend toward the mythic. They embody common, rather than personal, images of world and self. Approaching song from the point of view of communication leads to the perception of these images as "mythic" only in a limiting, negative way: song can hardly render anything else. Once we add the realization that the self enters some state in song, however, the description of such states as "mythic" is justified in a new way. Mythic images in song might have a formative, limiting, or sustaining relationship to individual self-perception. If the community's songs invite people into the interior of a shared image of what it is possible, inevitable, or desirable to be, the image is mythic in a positive and powerful sense. It is an element in the living mythology by which the community constitutes itself and its world.

If we return to the question of self-transcendence in song as Zuckerkandl raises it, with the added understanding of song words as mythic, we can see how important song words are. When music is song, the entrance to whatever music takes us into is configured as mythic image by the words in the song.

Songs are different from each other. Image implies definition and distinction, though it is a common speculation that all myths are somehow facets of some single unity: everything possible to be believed, said Blake, is an image of truth. Perhaps, in song, self-abandon is limited by the image given in the words, so that transcendence is less complete than other music can make it. Or perhaps song words make a constellation into which the self is projected so as to participate more easily but just as fully in that realm. To speak practically, there seem to be widely varying degrees to which singers and listeners lose themselves in songs. At the fullest, song experience like many other experiences is ecstatic: we are completely carried away. At lower degrees of release from self, the distinctness of the myth given by the words makes more difference. It makes more difference what song one is carried away in. The closer the myth lies to the surface of ordinary experience from which the song raises us, the more distinct and circumstantial and the less mythic it is, the more of selfhood there is in it.

Let us particularize this theoretical account a bit more. A song, let us suppose a blues lament, begins to be sung in our hearing. Some chance listeners feel the style of song has nothing to do with them, and for them it remains an object outside them in the world, the occasion for annoyance, curiosity, or indifference. Others respond. The first effect is an arrest of the normal vagaries of personal consciousness. The song is a distraction and an abstraction from such vagaries. Out of the welter of moods and states the listener is used to passing through, the music and the words draw up and give shape (perhaps in its details a relatively new, relatively unfamiliar shape—there is an indefinitely large bag of blues) to one mood, which preempts self-consciousness. The words that make this song pass through the mind. The voice that sings them does not make them the personal lament of this particular singer, though they are shaped and colored by the singer's vocal art. Neither do they become the listener's personal lament. They are transformed by the music into something not temporary and specific, something neither personal nor impersonal, that the singer and the listeners can (in Lehmann's phrase) live together. We participate. Perhaps the song is anecdotal, circumstantial, or it is strongly particularized by the power of the singer's personality; or on the other hand perhaps it is basic, universal; it easily lifts both the singer and us above our personal selves.

The song mentions things—an empty bed, a coffee grinder. We have seen that Zuckerkandl argues that song carries us into unity with objects as well as with other people. When we completely lose ourselves, there are no longer any separating relationships to anything. Through much of song experience relationships to things still seem to be present, although they are no longer ordinary relationships. Things are as mythic as selves in song. In the song I am thinking of here, Bessie Smith's "Empty Bed Blues," the bed, the coffee grinder, the cabbage and the bacon, all blur into earthy metaphors for the woman herself in remembered sex, and still they are casually evocative props. They do not need steady distinctness from her or from each other, or logical consistency as metaphors.

In song the particular facts of life do not need to be coped with. The things song disposes around us are ghosts. The attitude in which one indulges in a song is abstracted from real things it might be an attitude toward. Love, pity, or defiance of someone or something is replaced by the arrested posture of loving, pitying, or the like. The posture implies an object but the real object of the ordinary, contingent feeling is not there. It is for this reason that it seems false to sing a song to a real person as a communication. That person can tell there is a ghost, properly addressed by the song, intervening—and who is the message coming from? The perfunctory quality of communication in song words, with which we began this analysis, is a clue to, and finally a function of, this annihilation of relationships. Things in song, addressed or only mentioned, have being only as they are implied by the state of the subject. They remain implications, projections. The correlative here might be the toy called the Ghost Gun, which when pointed at a dark wall shines an image of its ghostly target there. We will see, in the buck and the bullock in "Sumer is icumen in," how lively such ghosts can be.

SONG AS TEXT

Song text is poetry; then again song is not poetry as we usually understand poetry, but rather a collateral descendant from a common ancestor. To examine and write about written text is suitable for the critic of poetry; the appropriateness of such an approach for the student of song is not so clear. Certainly to study song exactly as we study the superficially similar forms of written lyric poetry leads to gauche mistakes. The particular protocol of considering a given kind of song must emerge in the confrontation with an example of that kind of song. Before beginning practical criticism, however, general considerations, a general briefing for the critic of songs, can be gathered from the nature of song as it has been described here.

What the modern reader most wants to find in poetry is the poet's personal encounter with reality, fixed with subtle rightness in a unique construction of language. It should be clear that songs almost never answer to this expectation. Songs give us, for matter, something we can recognize; they present it in language sparing of surprises, consisting for the most part of well-chosen phrases rather than well-chosen words. This state of affairs deprives the poetry critic who addresses song verse of much of his normal project. The substance and expression of songs do not sustain the discriminative appreciation we have developed for poetry—that is, appreciation keyed to the distinctness of the verbal object from other similar objects. A song fulfills its potential in significant part according to what it shares with other similar good songs. In some styles this sharing may go to the extent of a borrowed chorus or stanza; in more styles, sharing of lines, images, and phrases testifies to the same fact: songs of a given kind for a given public converge upon received mythic images appropriate to the kind to which the songs belong, and the convergence shows in both thought and expression.

Song expresses and gives access to a state of experience. That is to say, it has a static quality. An effective song establishes directly the state it will sustain, and not much change can be introduced subsequently without a sense of breach. An English critic, Henry Raynor, writes that "song lyrics may *present* a situation or emotional experience, but must not explore or analyze it in terms that cannot be dealt with musically," that is, not with much articulation. Edward Doughtie comments:

> In a song lyric, although the images and ideas may be related to a central theme or an obvious central conceit, they tend to be isolated from each other; they accumulate rather than develop. Rarely, in fact, does an image or thought extend beyond two lines . . . the listener is rarely able to make connections of much complexity over a longer space of time.[35]

Elsewhere in his discussion Doughtie remarks that this iterative character of song lyrics accounts for the facts that singers can often omit stanzas without damage and that printed texts of the Elizabethan airs have transposed stanzas of certain poems. Bowra observes that in primitive song, "the lines, which are more or less independent units, can often be shuffled about and arranged in

different orders."[36] A glance at the variant forms of one of the
more common ballads in Child's collection shows gross differences in length between versions of a song that is still clearly the
same song. These examples testify to a fluidity in many kinds of
song text that baffles much of the structural analysis applied in
our time to poems.

This is not to say that songs are shapeless. We will see that
song texts can sometimes be parsed into elaborate patterns, particularly when they are the "texts" of preliterate song. The structures ordering songs are not, however, the subtle psychological
dramas of lyric poetry. The reader of Donne's "Canonization" or
Keats's "Ode to a Nightingale" is carried through intellectual and
emotional process. Literary criticism, as we will notice specifically in considering the Renaissance air, has recently become
interested in the psychodynamics of reader response to various
kinds of literature, a dynamics presupposing active, dramatic in-
teraction of the literature and the reader's intelligence. The experience of song lies distinctly aside from such process experience.
We might say that in place of such a psychodynamics of reading,
song criticism must assume, for singing and listening, a psychostatics. In words borrowed from one of T. S. Eliot's meditations,
we can say that song gives "Erhebung without motion." The experience accumulates rather than develops, and for this reason it
frustrates the effort to schematize it into dramatic pattern. The
patterns songs do show are common as opposed to unique, standing patterns as opposed to linear sequences of growth, evolution,
discovery, catharsis.

If we accept these cautions and press on to ask what meaning
and what value can be located in song text, it is best to raise the
question of the state of experience offered by the song, as that
state is inferable from the text. The constituent parts of the text,
its lines and stanzas, images, assertions of thought and feeling,
reports of events, performative gestures—all participate in and
sustain a state of experience that attentive criticism can illuminate as distinct from other comparable states and conversely as
akin to other states. The state is the implied content of the song.

The analytical understanding of it promises cultural and psychological insight into the life in which a song has its place. Song text has a documentary value that has not been fully appreciated.

The understanding of song offers also a more liberal sort of insight. A song text is the document of an occasion on which people of some time, place, and circumstance pause from their personal selves to enter into a common consciousness. Songs are different as time and place and circumstance differ where people seek to confirm what they are and what is. Songs offer them various congenial configurations of being, more or less local to the particulars of age, class, occupation, race, sex, or sect—less or more commonly human as they evoke common human feelings. Potential in every singing occasion is the passage through that configuration to knowledge of what transcends ourselves. It is not the business of criticism to trace this passage; but knowing that it is potential in everyone else's experience of songs as certainly as in our own is the ground of appreciative, fruitful, essentially educative criticism.

We may now return briefly to the lyric of Shakespeare's with which we began—not for a full new "reading" of it but to see how it may be understood as a song. In the first place we are free not to expect that the character Feste should be telling his personal story, any more than that Shakespeare should be telling his. Likewise, we do not need to look for a philosophical message cryptically withheld until we decode it, which would justify the song by showing that it does after all have information—sense—to convey.

No story and no lesson are conveyed. Rather a sketch of the most essential common story is evoked as present already to every listener, for the sake of a posture toward it. Even the sketch of the story is really no more than an evoked state: we can call it "having lived." It is not traced out in narrative sequence. It is present already in the first line. "When that I was and a little tine boy" gives what the rest of the song continues to give: rueful distance from childhood. The first extension of it, which makes little change, but as much as any other line, or stanza, is the next line after the refrain, "A foolish thing was but a toy." The line does not need translation or amplification. We can not so much comment on it as agree with it: yes, in those days, as not now, foolery was inconsequential.

The chorus lines have already begun their contribution in the first stanza. The contribution is not a matter of subtly varying commentary on the verses of succeeding stanzas. It is a recurring presence of the same proverbial acknowledgment. Its tone can be judged, I think, pretty confidently. It is like that of many proverbs. It poses the unaccommodating reality of the world of experience, somewhat negatively, but also (having paid it its due) with some wry satisfaction that it can be faced and managed. "Ah, well, into every life some rain must fall." Given a "heigh-ho" to go along with it, we have a clear, familiar, but subtle mix of acknowledging the negative facts of life, regretting them, placating them a little, and tossing them carelessly aside to affirm foolery anyway.

Each stanza admits the audience to the same participation, with the solitary fool on the empty comedy stage, in a kind of reverie between the play and the world. The last stanza breaks out of the pattern, returning to the business world of paid entertainers and their patrons. It performs the function called for by epilogue, but in changing the refrain and returning to "we" and "you," it is, strictly speaking, outside the song. The other stanzas are so much a unit, recurrence of the same whole in the present stanza each time, that their order and even their number do not make the song what it is. Appeal must be made to experience of it, but what we note here is enough to establish a poignant, appropriate, distinctive offering. Briefly and approximately, it can be described as a wry, wistful, jocular affirmation of clownish innocence, in a world suspicious of knavery: having lived in a rainy world, no longer as a child, still to be faithful, through the woeful consequences, to foolery.

To describe the song in this way is in part a reading of it but also something different. All this is not set up by its author as a story to be read, or packaged as a message from Shakespeare or Feste to the audience. Given music, the words are given the status music can give to words: when the clown sings them, he sings not to but for the audience. He tells them nothing they need to decode and learn. He evokes in them one of the ways of seeing life that they already have. Whoever is not Malvolio can enter it and share it.

Medieval Lyric as Song:
"Sumer is icumen in"

Words and music for "Sumer is incumen in." Thirteenth century. Harleian MS. 978. Courtesy of the British Library.

Svmer is icumen in. ✠
Lhude sing cuccu.
Groweþ sed and bloweþ med   [meadow]
and springþ þe wde nu.   [wood]
Sing cuccu

Awe bleteþ after lomb,   [ewe]
lhouþ after calue cu.   [lows, cow]
Bulluc sterteþ, bucke uerteþ.   [leaps, farts]
murie sing cuccu
Cuccu cuccu
Wel singes þu cuccu
ne swik þu nauer nu.   [don't stop]

Hanc rotam cantare possunt quatuor socij. A paucioribus autem
quam a tribus uel saltem duobus non debet dici preter eos qui
dicunt pedem. Canitur autem sic. Tacentibus ceteris unus inchoat
cum hijs qui tenent pedem. Et cum uenerit ad primam notam post
crucem; inchoat alius + sic de ceteris. singuli uero repausent ad
pausaciones scriptas +, non alibi; spacio unius longe note.

Sing cuccu nu. Sing cuccu.   Hoc repetit unus
quociens opus est.
faciens pausacionem
in fine

Pes

Sing cuccu. Sing cuccu nu.   Hoc dicit alius
pausans in medio &
non in fine. Sed im-
mediate repetens
principium

31

THIS SONG has come to be widely known to twentieth-century readers. It is one of the earliest lyrics we have that is written in language recognizable to readers of modern English,[1] if it is not actually the oldest survivor of all such lyrics, and among those oldest few it is easily the most accessible to us in spirit. Sir Arthur Quiller-Couch gave it the first place in his *Oxford Book of English Verse*, and Ezra Pound paid it the compliment of parody. More recently it has been given repeated attention by critics, in an outburst of critical studies of the medieval lyrics by English and American scholars during the past twenty-five years. Because it has been so thoroughly explicated as a lyric poem, it offers a good occasion for exploring the difference between poem and song.

Once a composition has been called a lyric poem, our romanticism is awakened. We expect lyric poetry to spring from and express very special experience. It may be the most characteristic response of modern readers of poetry to turn attention to the generation of the poem. We are fascinated by the power to create and by the conditions under which it works. We probe for origins with learned study of influences, traditions, and sources, seeking to establish the nature and limits of originality. When we read lyric poetry we are as curious about its genesis as children are about the genesis of babies. Thus some studies of this lyric have set about to hypothesize its origin.

> One morning on the southern countryside, the poet becomes suddenly aware of the arrival of joyous "sumer" (probably April). Realization comes in a moment so brief that he cannot hope by ordinary means to give concrete representation to the complex of impulses which unite almost as a single sense-impression to inform him of the happy fact. Nor can he by

conventional methods animate the symbols which have flashed
"sumer" upon his conscious mind.[2]

To respond in this way is to believe with Shelley that the mind in
creation is as a fading coal and that when composition begins inspiration is already on the decline. The moment of inspiration is
taken to be of primary worth and interest, the cynosure of critical
attention, and the writing as we have it to be a secondary approx-
imation. It is a lofty and even reverential idea of the poet, but it
has, I hope to show, peculiar demerits as an idea of songwriting,
not to speak of its naiveté with respect to the role of convention in
medieval writing. For any criticism, it poses the risk of fixation
upon that moment of inspired experience which we reach past the
text to grasp, wishing the writing itself out of our way.

For the purpose of keeping attention firmly on the work as it
exists in this world and not in another, hypothetical world, it will
be helpful to take the song itself and the live working of it to be
primary and to define the act of generating it to be not some effort
to catch the ineffable but only the task of willing and contriving a
song that works in such and such a way. This is not to imagine that
a writer begins with a job order and builds to it. Perhaps the song
really did burst forth in some poet's pasture. But if we deempha-
size the generation of it, which may have been a mystery to its
author and is certainly that to us, we will have attention free to
consider what the song does and gives.

Such a suggestion is the conventional wisdom of the old New
Criticism, but in proposing to avoid the generative thicket and the
intentional fallacy, I think it will still be useful here to indulge in
the affective fallacy, specifically for the reason that the object of
consideration is not poem but song. Careful analysis of the text
has been performed, and yet the song's life with music has not
been fully recognized by criticism. To understand the real nature
of the song we must not after all be content with the text as object
but must project it into performance and imagine the experience
it offers. It must be confessed that this procedure hazards opening
one door to fantasy after closing another, and perhaps it would be

most graceful to acknowledge that choosing to consider the audience's experience rather than the poet's is only a question of another perspective. But a song text is a script for a public event, and the nature of that event can at least as sensibly concern us as the psychology of the moment when the script was first thought of.

What might be gained from attending to the experience offered by the song to its audience may be suggested by the work of another critic who declines to attend to it and treats the text as lyric poem. The following is a portion of a note published in 1959 in *The Explicator*:

> Commentators have, in general, emphasized the objectivity of "Sumer is icumen in" and its twofold structure; they have praised the impersonal description of the arrival of spring as the speaker sees it manifest in the vegetable and animal worlds. . . . The speaker feels a delight in spring corresponding to that in the vegetable and animal worlds. . . . The actual song of the bird is a kind of reassurance for the speaker that it really is spring, thus climaxing the animal level and preparing for the intensity of the final lines. . . . And that the poet can present so personal a wish in such objective terms . . . is an indication of his art.[3]

Such an analysis as this, chastened by the warnings of Wimsatt and Beardsley, carefully severs the text-object from all speculation, taking it to be self-contained and essentially dramatic. A speaker, distinct from poet, is posited as the object of our scrutiny. The structures of the poem are the structures of his experience, and the poem wins admiration for its fine modeling of mental events. Intricate patterns of perception and emotion are wrought over each other.

But surely such structures, however undeniably they may exist as the text lies on the critic's desk, are evanescent in a singing of the song. In the present case we are prescribed by our manuscript source to take the song as a *rota*, a round or perpetual canon, where the words are sung over each other by up to six voices. It would be a frantic aesthete who sought to appreciate the patterns of psychological mimesis in the song, rising to "the intensity of the final lines," as the words danced circles around him. The song must be analyzed and understood not merely as structures in the two dimensions of paper but as words ordered to have their effect in vocal performance.

It has been asserted that the instructions for singing as we have them "do not fit the poem very well, and probably represent a late addition," and that the lyric may be "based on Welsh folk song," although the best dating from the manuscript and other contemporary documents now places both words and music around the middle of the thirteenth century.[4] But even if we suppose that there was once some other song, similar but simpler, we have this song delivered to us in an arrangement shown to be a happy one by modern performance and with the testimony that its transcriber knew it as specially suited to singing in a round. "This *rota*," he says, "can be sung by four. It should not be performed, however, by fewer than three, or at least by two, besides those who sing the burden." The text as we have it, with the words in whatever structures they may constitute, was not only sung, but sung in the playful contention of a round, with each line blurred by as many as five other simultaneous lines carried by other voices.

It is not necessary to complain that the verbal artistry of the lyric is willfully sunk into chaos by this musical arrangement. Such an argument might well be made, however, for the Latin verses that also appear on the manuscript, an alternative, homiletic text in the same meter:

Perspice christicola
que dignacio
Celicus agricola
pro vitis vicio
filio
non parcens exposuit
mortis exicio
qui captivos semivivos

a supplicio
vite donat
et secum coronat
in celi solio.

("Consider, christian—what an honor! The heavenly cultivator, because of a blemish in the vine, not sparing his son, exposed him to the destruction of death; who restores half-living prisoners from torment to life and crowns them together with himself on the throne of heaven.")

These lines come into the musical setting unequipped with any burden to take the place of "Sing cuccu nu. Sing cuccu. / Sing cuccu. Sing cuccu nu," but they would be embarrassed to borrow it. (Bertrand Bronson has suggested that the omission might be taken as an impish monastic joke.)[5] While they are singable, they march in a grand hypotactic arrangement (after the opening exclamation) from beginning to end, the second half a subordinate clause to the first, and are completely garbled by the overlapping of voices. Comparison of this pious impostor, to which we will return for fuller consideration later, with "Sumer is icumen in," shows that the text of the latter is a genuine song, which survives and flourishes in performance as a round. It is constructed in such a way that the arrangement in which we have it even extends and enhances the effects of the verses themselves.

To see how this can be so, it is necessary to understand how singer and audience experience words in the singing of any lyric. The singer, as I have argued in the introductory essay, in giving his own voice to the words makes them his own words; the audience takes the singer's voice to itself, and with it the words it delivers. There is little objective contemplation of the words but rather an appropriation of them, so that they sing through and for us. "Sumer is icumen in," if it is experienced as song rather than as printed poem, does not tell us that a certain poet celebrated spring but rather invites us to celebrate.

This is not simply to say that the audience moves into the

place of the poet, to chorus with him his tribute to spring, or that we move into the place of that hypothetical speaker to undergo the sequence of his feelings. If it happens that the day one sings or hears the song is a first blooming day of the new season, it is fair to say that the song might represent a greeting to the returning spring, which is what critics usually say about the lyric. But of course there is no need for such timing. While the lyric is clearly appropriate to a different time than, say, "Jingle Bells," it certainly need not be sung at the onset of spring. In 1972 Cat Stevens made a popular recording of Eleanor Farjeon's fine anthem "Morning Has Broken"; it was given wide radio play and was widely sold.[6] The text greets and celebrates morning, but surely only occasionally was the record heard at dawn, or even before noon. It offered its audience at any hour a few minutes of exultation in the spirit of sunrise. Now no one would claim that a painted sunrise should be contemplated only at daybreak. But since a song of dawn or spring so clearly infects us with a spirit of celebration like that with which we might really greet dawn or spring, there is a nagging inclination to confuse the real and ostensible occasions of such song. More especially, there is a tendency to confuse response to one with response to the other. "In its subject it is a *reverdie*, a song of joy in response to the glorious coming of spring," writes Edmund Reiss, "and few who know the lyric can help but feel the joy of life it reveals and respond to its exuberance . . ."; and later, "Through singing *cuccu*, man may be brought into the poem, and symbolically into nature, as he along with everything else celebrates life."[7] This is close to the truth, but it combines two unreliable assumptions: first, that an effective lyric must have been written, like "The Star-Spangled Banner," at the time of the heightened experience it reports; and second, that an audience, being shown the scene that supposedly stirred the original excitement, can be drawn into it to achieve vicariously the same excitement.

The first of these ideas is the generative fallacy again. The second assumes that we respond to singing as we generally think we respond to reading, by seeing something flashed on the mind's

eye. But this proposition is doubtful. It leads Reiss to the awkward concept of "audial imagery": "Line 8 continues this audial
imagery, though here our attention shifts from the mother-child
groupings to the adolescent males eager to show their prowess."[8] I
do not think that anything much like this happens when the song
is performed, if only because everything happens so quickly.

Awe bleteth after lomb,
Lhouth after calve cu.
Bulluc sterteth, bucke verteth.
Murie sing cuccu.

Consider two possibilities. Perhaps, hearing the song, I see
vividly before me germinating seeds, flowering meadow, cattle,
sheep, bullock and buck, and hear vividly the onomatopoetic
sounds of animals and bird, and I enter into that scene and experience the writer's original rush of joy. Or perhaps, and I think
this is more true to experience, in singing or hearing the song I
indulge myself at its invitation in a lively, somewhat silly liberation from objective attention to anything, which we may as well
still call "celebration of life"—but with a distinction of *celebration* as transitive (celebrating something) from this *life-celebration*
as intransitive, without object. It is not that the song is irrelevant
to spring, or is nonsense. The quality of the celebration is specifically appropriate to spring, cued by the announcement of the
opening line. Spring songs are an enduring convention; the medieval audience knew and we know what romp we are invited to.
One may come to the song, or it may come to mind, because one
is in the right spring spirit for it. But though we know before and
during the song what occasion it claims for its warrant, it does not
refer outward to real spring once it is under way. It puts on a revel
that includes us. We are already in it when other figures make
their appearance, and we are not responding specifically to them
upon visualizing them. They enter as the right props, making
gestures that help us sustain the revel. While we catch these
glimpses of visual images, we are much more insistently bom-
barded by audial effects, which are not the sounds of the barnyard

but the sounds of song. A quick *lhouth* is not much like the low-ing of a cow and is much less striking a sound in any case than the purely auditory, nonreferential pattern of "Groweth sed and blow-eth med" or of "Bulluc sterteth, bucke verteth."

The most insistent sound is the nonsense sound of *cuccu*, which certainly is onomatopoetic, mimetic in origin. But it does not continue to be mimetic. Various meditational practices are built on the fact that any word sheds its sense upon a small num-ber of consecutive repetitions. *Cuccu*, which sounds silly in human speech anyway, quickly becomes in the song a Tra la la. Reiss makes the ingenious suggestion that it might have brought into the medieval mind an association with the verb *cukken*, "to void excrement," given the neighborhood of *verteth*—in which case attention is further drawn aside into silly play, a long way from that "reassurance" to the rapt poet on the farm. Reiss also gives the sound a serious function: "Through singing *cuccu*, man may be brought into the poem. . . . The sound *cuccu* may thus be seen possessing a magical quality, as though the repetition of it can bring about a certain desired condition. . . . Here the sound *cuccu* acts both to memorialize and to create the *sumer* that is *icu-men in*."[9]

It is true that the sound *cuccu* is part of the magic that lifts us into celebration in the song. It is misleading to say that it memo-rializes or creates summer. As it sheds referential value it sheds its ability to remind us of anything or to conjure up anything. It contributes rather to a pure state of cheery and inattentive levity. Reiss underestimates the magic that *cuccu* works in the song be-cause he sees it only six times in the two stanzas, followed by a refrain: "It is this perpetual sound that comes forth noticeably in the final two lines. These comprise a quasi-refrain and seem to be in response to the imperative 'Ne swik thu naver nu' . . ." But this statement is not right, for there are no such final two lines; he refers to the burden. E. K. Chambers and Frank Sidgwick are equally misleading in printing them as lines 1–2, and Quiller-Couch even more so in printing them as the second half of a quatrain where the lyric splits into thirds.[10] They are given by the manuscript as a tumbling background to the whole song, on top of each other on top of the superimposed lines of the stanzas. If one wishes to parse the lyric out into a lyric poem about spring, the lines have no place at either beginning or end, any better than between stanzas or even between lines.

We have invoked the *rota* structure, but that structure need not be considered to see how the lyric works. Even without the incessant chant of *cuccu* in the background, "Sumer is icumen in" works as a self-contained occasion for indulging in joyful levity, appropriate to spring but not primarily representational of it. The stanzas have their effects by sound, patterned heavily over the images embodied in the words. Like much successful song verse, and drastically unlike the unwieldy Latin poem attached to the same music, the lines are elementally simple in syntax, curt, and almost completely independent of each other, except that they work together toward cumulative effect. They pass along little thought from one to another but catch attention each within itself by alliteration and assonance:

Sumer (i)s (i)cumen (i)n
Lhude sing cuccu.

Reiss traces several patterns beyond the obvious ones.[11]

The reduplicative form of the motif-word *cuccu* is approximated by the form of the two most memorable lines, or pairs of semilines, "Groweth sed and bloweth med," and "Bulluc sterteth, bucke verteth." The first consists of a doubly rhyming pair of trisyllables balanced on *and*; the second echoes each of its first four syllables in its second four, except that in the two second syllables the *k* sound begins one and ends one. Such ingenious engineering produces a strong rocking effect, an effect of motion interrupted and returned upon its course, like the swing of a pendulum. Lines that somehow return upon themselves are a very widely used device of songwriters. They are often used with the cognate musical devices that give the name to rock music, at least when rock is taken as the rocking and rolling music in which each beat is rebounded by backbeat. The tight swing of such lines of verse contains a kinetic energy, a very real energy that moves heads and shoulders even without music. The effect is motion in place, as is also the related effect of alliteration, as with the *l* sounds in "Awe bleteth after lomb / Lhouth after calve cu," though the motion suggested by alliterative lines seems closer to spinning than to oscillation. Such effects build up a state of mental and bodily excitement, the state the song offers us to indulge in, supported but not aroused directly or simply by the subject and what the lyric says about it.

It is because the lines of "Sumer is icumen in" work this way that we can say that the *rota* arrangement does no violence to the effective verbal structures of the verse, and even extends and amplifies their effects. As the lines swirl through their dance, attention catches them whole as short independent units but is continually interrupted in following the sequence of the stanza by notice of another intersecting voice. Notice is happily deflected from one place in the sequence to another, from one glimpsed image to another, none distinct for long from the whirl of the dance. The experience is akin to giddiness, and does not favor objective aesthetic contemplation. The excited state in which it catches us up is joyfulness on the ostensible occasion of spring, but it is an excitement belonging to the song itself. The song offers us an occasion to concentrate and indulge the feelings in us that are associated with the signs of spring, picking us up like Dorothy out of Kansas in a whirl of words.

"Sumer is icumen in" works as a song, but "Perspice christicola," the Latin poem on the same manuscript page, does not. The text of the secular lyric can keep its essential sense for singers and listeners even in a round, while the Latin church text can hardly do so. Unfortunately for clear definitions, there is every likelihood that the monks who sang one sang the other. "Perspice christicola" falls outside the area in which our analysis of song makes sense. Either the analysis calls for modification, or this text-with-music must be placed in some neighboring but different area, not song but something else.

The analysis of songs offered in the introduction begins from a communicational model of song experience, where words work to bring across some message. That model is most helpful in showing what songs cannot be or do. To describe positively the quality of song experience we have had recourse to a less objective scheme. The notion of transmitting and receiving between one of us and another may actually be too simple for fully describing anything we do with words. Walter Ong writes:

> In the last analysis, the medium is not even a medium, something in between. Words destroy in-betweenness, put me in your consciousness and you in mine. There is no adequate analogue for verbalization. Verbalization is ultimately unique. True information is not "conveyed."[12]

The transmission-reception model for songs fits best in the case of a performance by a singer or singers for an audience that does not know the song or expect to learn it but takes it for the entertainment of the present. In such cases we can speak of the performer's technique as his "delivery," implying that he brings us something with his voice. Such a relationship of performer to audience is fairly special: it is generally not found in folk music or in art music, in both of which the repertoire is for the most part known to its audience. It also is not the case with contemporary popular music performed on record or tape. It is essentially a stage relationship, realized in the season's new shows in musical theater. Most of the songs considered in this book, including "Sumer is icumen in," imply some more complicated relationship of words to consciousness than that the words are simply received and registered.

Examination of "Sumer" shows a verbal construct beautifully adapted to conditions very unpromising for conveyance of information. It would probably be claiming too much to say that the lyric, heard for the first time, will deliver its semantic goods under the conditions of performance. More safely it can be said that "Sumer" will keep for us the sense that we know it has. If the informational model is retrenched in this way, we are no longer asking the song to bring anything but minimal cues across the space presumed by communication, especially from singers to listeners. In the mind of the singer, the text answers its function by being constructed to offer, in local stretches, separately functional members of the verbal scaffolding of the distinctive experience structure of this song.

"Perspice christicola" still fails to be songlike. If song is only asked to cue for us the realization of some familiar mood-state or mind-set, by successive verbal phrases, "Perspice christicola" may be suspected not to be up to the task. Once the text is subjected to the centrifuge effect of performance in round, the hypotactic complications of what it says are too great for bits of verbal phrases even to remind us of their full message when we already know it.

The circle to which this setting of the Latin lyric properly belongs is one in which the relationship of music to text, and, more fundamentally, of audience to text, is different from the relationships assumed in what is here understood as song. The origins of the art it represents can be traced to the emergence of the motet form out of the *conductus* at the beginning of the thirteenth century.

The earliest forms of polyphonic music, through the *conductus*, set one text at a time. With the motet, composers began to give differing texts to the different voices—sometimes in different languages and sometimes with no relation to each other whatever. Ernest H. Sanders describes the *conductus* as "a setting of poetry in which the chief function of the music can be compared to manuscript illumination; the upper parts decorate the tune and, together, they decorate the text." But the motet structures are

basically not accompanied songs or duets, "expressing" the text(s). The role of poetry in a medieval motet is best defined by analogy with the stained-glass windows in a Gothic church. . . . The music does not accompany, elucidate or intensify; but the poetry illuminates and reflects the structure of the music.[13]

What is presumed by the motet form is also presumed when "Perspice christicola" is committed to round. The poem is set into an orderly and musically pleasing structure in which it cannot be coherently heard. Whether as here a single discursive text is reflected onto itself, or as in the motets two texts share time with a bit of a third and deprive each other of intelligibility, what happens in this stage of polyphony is that the words are set into the music without concern over whether they are recoverable. That this is so is shown by what is set. Single-text forms found in manuscripts with motets set texts clearly intended to be heard. Sanders says, "The poetic texts of the *conductus* were never intended as entertainment; they were devotional, homiletic, ceremonial, or ancillary to the liturgy."[14] When the motet appears, this earnestness diminishes. Dom Anselm Hughes traces the evolution:

> The purest type of early motet consists of a liturgical tenor with the two upper parts singing . . . a trope upon the words of the tenor. . . .
>
> Later on . . . the Latin is discarded in favour of the vernacular in one upper voice only, while the other, with no apparent sense of incongruity, retains the church text in the original Latin. . . . When this practice is attempted in church, however, we are not surprised to find that the ecclesiastical authorities denounce it as improper, for the French texts are with a few exceptions frankly secular and deal for the most part with lovers and their lasses.[15]

There is no concern that the texts will clash with each other, because neither text is coming across. On the other hand, there are cases where the texts are relevant to each other, in a pattern of hierarchy or of mutual commentary. In such cases the significance of their juxtaposition, which is crafted into the musical composition, is much too complex to be evident in performance. Like the careful setting of *Death* to a black note by later composers, it is a significance intellectually apprehensible in the knowing of the work but not in the hearing of it.

The knowing implicit here is an essentially visual mode of knowing, specifically reading. The significance of its presumption in the music of the thirteenth century is that the culture to which that music belongs is a culture profoundly oriented toward written text. Walter Ong, a pioneering scholar of such distinctions, remarks that "medieval culture is a transitional culture, oral-aural at root but scriptural in bent."[16] In particular, the clerical culture that produced and sang "Perspice christicola" was a culture defined by its veneration of written text—scripture. In the midst of generally illiterate Europe, the monks of institutions like Reading Abbey, where the "Sumer"-"Perspice" manuscript was preserved, treasured and labored at writing. Over against the lay populace, they understood, and thought in terms of, what could be and had been written down.

This culture was the first for which music was something written. It created the first systematic musical notation. It evolved the idea of a written score and combined its written music with written words. Eventually it devised the motet, named by a latinization of the French *mot*, "word." A writer of the time, Johannes de Grocheo, explained the form and commented:

> This type of song . . . is not suitable for the common people, because they neither sense its subtleties nor are they delighted when listening to it. But it is fitting for the educated and for those who seek the refinements of the arts.[17]

The common people would never see the written music calculated for the written text. No matter how musical they might be, they had no susceptibility to the distinctively two-dimensional constructs of this written music, where the precisely measured horizontal phrasing of each voice is mapped vertically against the other voices and where the balance and order of the whole manifests and celebrates a mathematical harmony.[18]

The integrity and the significance of such a text as "Perspice christicola" is to be known through reading. For the culture to which it belongs, the lyric is endowed with integrity and significance by virtue of the fact that it has been written, and it will carry the air of integrity and significance with it whatever becomes of it. If it is broken into bits by musical arrangement, it will still be text.

This is not to say that the text will be brought whole to mind when heard. In performance it will carry, not its discursive significance, but the assurance that it has one. (Performers might sing from separate parts and not even see, themselves, the grand design.) The privileged status of the written word in medieval clerical society gives the text a special security: it exists prior to its musical setting and is not vulnerable to that setting, as words would be that came into existence primarily for the sake of the musical performance. It can be looked up, before, during, or after a singing, and it will not fail to be intact.

Motet or round can incorporate written texts, whether scriptural or ecclesiastical or secular, for any purpose that pleases the artist who puts the musical whole together, without anxiety that they will become meaningless. From the most sober point of view, the divine ordering of the world is devoutly celebrated with the construction of an intricate whole out of meaningful parts, whether or not the significance of parts is occult to the observer of the whole. When the use of the techniques is merely playful and fully secular, on the other hand, the same security invests the text: playfulness always implies security. The word can be treated freely because it is not constrained by its oral-aural responsibilities.

In the perception of the performer of the music, the single voice moves through the composition free to delight in separate but unalienated motion, dancing, but within choreography. Participation in strictly right order also involves passing encounters, separations, pursuits, and approaches. A modern singer of polyphony described the excitement of following her line in descent to meet a surfacing lower voice as almost sexual. With all this going on the words can count on little attentiveness to their sense. Since they are certified as essentially and permanently significant by appearing somewhere on paper, they do not need it.

Dance and Game Song:
"Holly and Ivy"

Nay, Ivy, nay, hyt shal not be, iwys;   [certainly]
Let Holy hafe the maystry, as the maner ys.

Holy stond in the hall, fayre to behold;
Ivy stond without the dore; she ys ful sore a-cold.

Nay, Ivy, nay, hyt shal not be, iwys;
Let Holy hafe the maystry, as the maner ys.

Holy and hys mery men, they dawnsyn and they syng;
Ivy and hur maydenys, they wepyn and they wryng.

Nay, Ivy, nay, hyt shal not be, iwys;
Let Holy hafe the maystry, as the maner ys.

Ivy hath a kybe; she kaght yt with the cold;   [chilblain]
So mot they all haf ae that with Ivy hold.

Nay, Ivy, nay, hyt shal not be, iwys;
Let Holy hafe the maystry, as the maner ys.

Holy hat berys as rede as any rose;
The foster, the hunters kepe hem fro the doo.   [forester; doe]

Nay, Ivy, nay, hyt shal not be, iwys;
Let Holy hafe the maystry, as the maner ys.

Ivy hath berys as blake as any slo;
Ther com the oule and ete hym as she goo.

Nay, Ivy, nay, hyt shal not be, iwys;
Let Holy hafe the maystry, as the maner ys.

Holy hath byrdys, a ful fayre flok,
The nyghtyngale, the poppynguy, the gayntyl lavyrok.   [lark]

Nay, Ivy, nay, hyt shal not be, iwys;
Let Holy hafe the maystry, as the maner ys.

Gode Ivy, what byrdys ast thou?
Non but the howlat, that kreye, "How, how!"

Nay, Ivy, nay, hyt shal not be, iwys;
Let Holy hafe the maystry, as the maner ys.

HESE VERSES come from a manuscript of the mid-fifteenth century, one of two versions of this song that have been found. They are printed with discussion of the folklore behind them by Richard L. Greene in his collections of the early English carols.[1] They compose a Christmas carol, in the strict medieval sense in which a carol has stanzas and choral burden as here, deriving ultimately from the singing pattern of the carole, or ring-dance. The carole was a popular pastime in England into the sixteenth century, not exclusively but especially at the Christmas holiday season. This example shows its tie to Christmas by its use of the holly and ivy emblems, which as midwinter greenery are extensively twined into Christmas ritual.

We do not know whether or not any given carol text that survives to us was sung in carole dance. This text seems to imply, as Greene suggests, some sort of holiday "barring-out" dance game, in which the men playfully exclude the women. Of that game we know nothing except what the song says.

The song teases the excluded Ivy and her party of maidens. We may distinguish the abuse it lays upon the females from the antifeminist literature of the Middle Ages, known to modern readers who are friends of the Wife of Bath. There is nothing com-

plaining or argumentative against women here. No case is made
against women, no scoring of points in the world's ordinary sexual
strife. It is not imputation of fault but exultation over default. It is
pure and cheerful insult, "mery" in tone, with a kind of jolly
malice.

This sort of thing clearly needs a special occasion—not that
abuse is not possible, or even natural, in the regular course of
things, but that this triumphant tone clearly makes no accommodation to resistance or reprisal and is thus unworldly. It is of
course a jest and a game, which are both special occasions on
which we license the expression or exercise of impulses normally
dressed up or held in by social restraint. This is holiday song,
song for a day of indulgence and license, with everyday rules set
aside. We are not used to finding such opportunities for shaking
off inhibition in Christmas carols today, but kissing under the
mistletoe and office-party indulgence continue very central traditions of Christmas as a time of license.[2] "Holly and Ivy" is a jest,
in a song, in a game, on a holiday, such that men may give vent in
a refined, channeled, purified form to the lust for *maystry*, without real-world repercussions.

The game-dance-song recognizes men and women only as the
followers of their respective plant-symbol figures, not as either individuals or as mere sexes. Both Holly and Ivy, for their parts, are
now human and now botanical, dancing or suffering chilblains
and again, bearing berries and accommodating birds. The double
nature of Holly echoes the transformation of the dance leader into
the god who sponsors or inspires him in the ancient Greek *molpê*
and indeed in primitive ritual dance in general.[3] Here it may
stand for us as the protective investiture into role, a costume, as it
were, for the blameworthy instigator of this deplorably abusive
game. He is recognizably male and yet safely nonhuman. Behind
him dance his party, and with Ivy cower her party.

The song does not allow us to identify these parties as simply
the sexes. The imprecation of the *kybe* is for those who "with Ivy
hold." The sex line as the party line is disturbed further in the B
text:

So wold I that every man had that with Yvy will hold.

Even if *man* here is taken to be indefinite and genderless, still the parties of the game seem to be made up of choosers and adherents, not necessarily all men and all women. Since the game at least pretends a great, invidious difference of the two parties, to hold with Holly and join in to the dance, to spurn Ivy in the repeated burdens and testify the natural *maystry* of Holly, is to take a significant step beyond simple maleness. To carry the question of what sort of step it is any further, we must ask why this particular game should be a Christmas game. Among the various urges that might hope for indulgence on the holiday, what case is there for masculine mastery?

Widely scattered scraps of British folklore identify Christmas as the time when an unlucky misstep can curse a house with a year of female domination.[4] Why should these threshold customs, many employing these same emblems of holly and ivy for male and female, accumulate around Christmas, as opposed to, say, New Year's Day, when we are more used to raising questions and hopes concerning the fortunes of the coming year? In the specific case of our carol-game, the exile of women, weeping, on the day of the nativity might be associated with the taboo of childbirth, but such a speculation would be of no help in accounting for the question of dominance that is agitated by this song and by the patterns of Christmastime folk superstitions.

It seems more satisfactory to take guidance here from the burden of the song, which reiterates that ascendancy of Holly is customary, "as the maner ys," as the verses attempt to assert that it is natural, and further, to deny some implicit challenge or counterclaim, *reasserting* dominance:

Nay, Ivy, nay, hyt shal not be, iwys;
Let Holy hafe the maystry, as the maner ys.

The counterclaim at Christmas is to be found in the tableau of the nativity. Christmas is the hour of glory of mother and infant. It is woman who presents salvation to the world, and without male help, because the woman's merit is greater than the merit of any man. Woman is at the center of the stage, enshrined, while various men kneel in awe and submission at the periphery. Even the ox and ass are closer to the center of things.

English men and boys of the fifteenth century and earlier were as firmly impressed as Christians of other times and places have been with this geometry of the nativity. Much of our modern image of nativity scenes derives from Italian and north European paintings. England had little similar painting to show the faithful, but other representations of the cynosure mother and cradle were common. In the cathedrals were some stained-glass nativities (as well as other arrangements giving central place to Mary, such as Assumptions and the great centripetal "Tree of Jesse" window at York), perhaps some whole crèche scenes, and certainly liturgical plays like the *Pastores*:

> Let a manger be prepared at the back of the altar, and let a figure representing the Holy Mary be placed in [*sic*] it.[5]

The nearest priests are dressed up like midwives.

This humiliation of men is mysterious and unique, and not customary, not what the *maner* is. It is a good idea not to let it get out of hand, not to let it precipitate a shift in domestic politics: in company with about one bad omen, it might be enough to upset the normal scheme of things in any given house for the whole year. So those men who are willing to rouse themselves may step into such a dance as "Holly and Ivy" and react. The reaction must be cautious, of course. It is no good taking exception to the mystery of the nativity itself, and the grievance of the occasion cannot come to the surface. Where we can find it is in the implicit shape of the game-dance.

Holy stond in the hall, fayre to behold;
Ivy stond without the dore; she ys ful sore a-cold.

Like most of the dances associated with the carol, this dance is a ring, an excluding ring. Men are in, women are out. Where the warm, dry, bright, snug, joyful center of things is, where the madonna and cradle were, there the men have their dance. The women can have the outside, the dark, and the cold.

Actually this reactionary state of things is not really what the manner is, either. The game fantasy is an unworldly, holiday pretense. What does it really pretend? A correspondent of *Notes and Queries* in 1896 found the symbolism of the song strange, and "stranger still why the weeping ivy is placed without the door and the dancing holly within, a position which the youngest Viking, the beardless boy, would have scouted and contemned."[6] The solution he proposed, that we "accept the holly and ivy as the memorials of the return of the exiled Goths from the borders of the Euxine," does not further the present inquiry. But the sense that there is something peculiar about the men's claiming the snug indoors remains.

That claim seems to mime a return to a paradise, where deprivation, pain, weeping, and the possibility of sexual experience are put outside the gates. One version of that fantasy is sometimes argued to be nostalgia for the womb—which the hall fairly comfortably symbolizes—in which case the objection that this cozy security would be scorned by real men and even by little men is bypassed by the regression beyond the age of beardless boys, back to prenatal comfort, or at least to the neonatal snugness of the manger, the only place at the center of the nativity tableau open to any male.

The dance of Holly and his party, taunting and rejecting Ivy, cleaving to themselves and claiming this womb or nursery or clubhouse, is not merely reactionary but regressive. Its impetus is obscure jealousy of woman and baby, and it offers a separatist play fantasy where there is no challenge allowed because no challenger can come in. It is the Peter Pan solution.

Oral Ballad:
"The Bitter Withy"

As it fell out on a Holy day
   The drops of rain did fall, did fall,
Our Saviour asked leave of His mother Mary
   If He might go play at ball.

"To play at ball, my own dear Son,
   It's time You was going or gone,
But be sure let me hear no complaint of You
   At night when You do come home."

It was upling scorn and downling scorn,
   Oh, there He met three jolly jerdins:
Oh, there He asked the three jolly jerdins
   If they would go play at ball.

"Oh, we are lords' and ladies' sons,
   Born in bower or in hall,
And You are but some poor maid's child
   Born'd in an ox's stall."

"If you are lords' and ladies' sons
   Born'd in bower or in hall,
Then at the very last I'll make it appear
   That I am above you all."

Our Saviour built a bridge with the beams of the sun,
   And over it He gone, He gone He,
And after followed the three jolly jerdins,
   And drownded they were all three.

It was upling scorn and downling scorn
   The mothers of them did whoop and call,
Crying out, "Mary mild, call home your Child,
   For ours are drownded all."

Mary mild, Mary mild, called home her Child,
  And laid our Saviour across her knee,
And with a whole handful of bitter withy
  She gave Him slashes three.

Then He says to His Mother, "Oh, the withy! oh! the withy,
  The bitter withy that causes me to smart, to smart,
Oh! the withy it shall be the very first tree
  That perishes at the heart."

HE BITTER WITHY" eluded Francis James Child when he made his great edition of the British ballads. Reported to scholars late in the nineteenth century, it was officially captured and put on display only in the twentieth. It is, however, a certified traditional ballad, having ranged free in oral tradition until written down in 1888 from the singing of a man about seventy, who had it from his grandmother.[1] His report alone puts it at large in the eighteenth century, and its form suggests that it can claim the same obscure antiquity as the ballads brought together by Child, or before him by Thomas Percy and Walter Scott.

This peculiar narrative of a rather spiteful boy Jesus may seem to us now either deplorable or charmingly irreverent—not Sunday school material. But the story belongs to a family of anecdotes attached to the childhood of Jesus by the apocryphal gospels; the relevant texts were compared by Gordon Gerould shortly after the ballad was first printed. He showed that the story told here is built of elements widely distributed in medieval Europe, in which, for example, the boy Jesus hangs his water-pitcher on a sunbeam, or performs feats that other children imitate to their

own harm. Variants were attached to the stories of other prank-
ster-heroes. Gerould prints an analogous exploit by Tom Thumb
from a seventeenth-century chapbook:

Of whom to be reueng'd, he tooke
  (in mirth and pleasant game)
Black pots and glasses, which he hung
  vpon a bright sunne-beame.
The other boyes to doe the like,
  in pieces broke them quite;
For which they were most soundly whipt,
  Whereat he laught outright.[2]

The first four stanzas of the ballad are closely followed in a carol,
"The Holy Well," found in an eighteenth-century broadside, with
a didactically pious sentiment given to the child savior in his response to social ostracism. The carol is probably derivative from
the ballad, representing an effort to make something useful and
uplifting out of it.

   "The Bitter Withy" shows clearly the pattern associated with
the ballads that was described by F. B. Gummere as "incremental
repetition." When Jesus is told in stanza four,

"Oh, we are lords' and ladies' sons,
  Born in bower or in hall,
And You are but some poor maid's child
  Born'd in an ox's stall,"

his reply in stanza five uses the wording of the first two lines as
the first two lines of his retort:

"If you are lords' and ladies' sons
  Born'd in bower or in hall . . ."

Stanza seven reuses the odd and perhaps garbled phrasing "It was
upling scorn and downling scorn" that opens stanza three, as the
mothers trace the path of the playing children. In the same stanza
the mothers appeal, "Mary mild, call home your Child," and

when she duly does in the next stanza the narrative repeats the words, as "Mary mild, Mary mild, called home her Child."

This repetition of phrasing in successive stanzas, where small modification adapts the words to a new use or effect, is the signature of the oral ballad.[3] It is a versatile device and generates a variety of strong effects, including smart or bitter repartee, dramatic suspense, and an air of implacable fatality. It is not merely a stylistic convention. It is logically related to the nature of the ballads as orally composed and orally transmitted: the pattern is mnemonic—presumably for the maker, certainly for the singer who must also be the rememberer even if he is the remaker.

Like the other traditional ballads, "The Bitter Withy" belongs to an audience that is illiterate. It is popular song, not merely intended for wide popularity like modern pop song, but of the people, by the people, for the people; and the inference from its form is substantiated by what it says. The song has clear class prejudices. It offers its audience indulgence in a fantasy of revenge upon snobs. The disappointment of the boy Jesus in his search for playmates is specifically a rebuff of lowly by lordly, generated by upper-class arrogance in the boys he meets. (The appearance of the puzzling nonce-word "jerdins" to name the boys signals feeling—apparently invidious feeling, to judge by the context—toward them, interfering with mere objective naming of them.)

It is not clear that the song's proprietary audience thinks that young lords should play with peasant lads: we will return to this point in a moment. The song converts the attitudes, and perhaps even the obligations, of their social standing into the unequivocally damnable gesture of rejecting Jesus, so that they are victimized for being who they are. The fantasy is sheer grudging aggression. The odd wording of the stage-setting line, "It was upling scorn and downling scorn," if it is not an accurate transmission of a forgotten locution, may be a garbling of some other way of saying "up and down, here and there," by the interference of *scorn* as a sort of spirit hanging about in the song, both in the sneering attributed to the young lords and in the callous indifference returned upon their drowning and their mothers' grief. Scorn, any-

way, is what the song offers us to feel in requital for the insult of
the young scorners, when their drownings are only worth a
spanking.

It is important for understanding the attitudes built into the
ballad to see that it does not have what might be called a demo-
cratic spirit. There is nothing subversive about it. On the contrary, it is thoroughly accepting of hierarchy. It imagines only the
changing of places.[4] The young lords scorn Jesus, and he un-
cloaks himself to reveal one of such supernal rank that he can
scorn them in turn:

"Then at the very last I'll make it appear
    That I am above you all."

If anything, it is their decision to play with him after all that is
their undoing. The carol adapted from the ballad has Jesus sadly
declining vengeance (damnation!) on his scorners, and such restraint makes the sin of hurting his feelings stand out awkwardly,
emphasizing the lesson of humility. Here Jesus gives better than
he gets, triumphing where he was triumphed over, in a small pre-
view of Judgment Day. The counterblow wipes out the offense,
and we are left not offended with the young lords but only smugly
satisfied at their downfall. Dealing out humiliation is the game
being played in these verses. If there were a lesson (really no lesson is being taught) it would have to be to be careful to deal out
humiliation only to the vulnerable party, only downwards. Indeed
the game continues beyond the drowning. The next move is that
Jesus is punished.

The notion of the sinless Christ-child being spanked like another child, which according to Gerould has been found at least
once elsewhere in medieval representation, is an odd one. The
words insist on the incongruity: "laid our Saviour across her
knee." The idea is amusing, and the amusement it entails seems
to be the sort of humor that springs from the momentary triumph
over something feared. Jesus is regarded with some ambivalence
in the ballad. He is powerful, even dangerous, like other folklore
semideities to which he is approximated by the story. He is also,

like the trickster-hero figures of folklore, the wish-fulfillment identification figure who gets back at what we hate and fear: he is us. But the good joke on the rich young lords goes too far, and the audience has been given excessive indulgence in the fantasy of getting back; or perhaps it is only that any such fantasy must be crossed by a gesture of contrition, however formal and trivial, in deference to one's reality sense, to the higher imposed layers of socialized personality. So Jesus must be spanked. We are a little afraid of him and his power. But he is also somehow us, our stand-in. It must be that we are a little afraid of the impulse in ourselves to strike back, knowing the practical dangers of doing it. The fantasy aggression must be tempered with a gesture of self-reproof, because on the whole, or at least on the surface, we are not in favor of getting even.

"The Bitter Withy" accepts the game of giving back what you get, aggression for aggression, and the game does not end with the spanking either. Christ of the Gospels taught a law of forgiveness; but this boy Jesus is a pre-Christian Jesus, a preadult and presocial trickster. So while Mary must give him a reproof, he need not accept it; and since any gesture of aggression returned directly on Mary mild is, if anything, more outlandish an idea than a spanking for the savior, Jesus curses the instrumental withy.

The curse on the withy is a very neat resolution for the song. Gerould regarded it as adventitious to the legendary anecdote, yet it is such a happy twist that we could equally well argue that it is the kernel of the whole story, the place it begins. With this ending "The Bitter Withy" is a just-so story, a half-serious etiological myth. Consider the logic of the storyteller who begins with the challenge of why the withy trees along the watercourses tend to rot out. Perhaps they are under some curse. Now who could have anything against a withy, the tree of wands and switches? A boy. What boy small enough to be spanked might have power to curse? Jesus, of course, who cursed a fig tree in scripture. How can we imagine Jesus needing to be spanked? He has done some mischief, short of sin: nothing showing evil will in himself, hence something provoked. Who would we like to cast as the provoker?

What mischief does fantasy most want the secretly omnipotent child of the carpenter to commit?

Approaching the ballad in this backward fashion offers one further, or one alternative, possible understanding of the function of the song for its audience. The traditional ballads often tell grim tales of bloody or uncanny events. Capturing such events in narrative, fitting them to melody, and telling them to ourselves in the repetition of familiar song, deals with the menace of such events to some minimum extent. Fearful things happen, we say, and especially if we say it in proverb or song, we are mastering, containing, the fearfulness. "The Bitter Withy" seems quite light-hearted, except as it reports casualties, and we have no sympathy for them. But insofar as the song, however lightly, explains away what might be imagined as the working of a curse, it deprecates and manages the anxiety we may very well feel about the possible descent of occasional unaccountable curses. In such a legend as "The Bitter Withy" gives us, we have said above, the boy Jesus is a little alarming. Divine power strikes out from him in ways that the everyday world cannot be comfortable with. In some sense the audience takes that display of power to be believable and imagines it exercised in the way the audience's own impulses would direct. But if on any level, from simple credulity to something much more elusive, we accept the possibility of such unaccountable power at large in the world, the song will help us in our uneasiness over the workings of that power. Freud suggested that dreams may function sometimes to reassure us by positing manageable cases of possible disasters, as when one dreams of failing an examination or a course once one has safely passed it. The curse on the withy might work that way: among the curses of the world, it is an acceptable curse.

So far the analysis of "The Bitter Withy" does not distinguish the ballad much from a folktale. Many of the traditional ballads have sister folktales; "The Bitter Withy" might well be transprosed out of its music and versification, and still it would keep most of the character visible in its narrative as it stands. The experience it offers specifically as song is nevertheless distinct from what a prose version could render, and the distinction requires some attention.

To make prose out of this verse would be to loosen its orderings into some more subtle morphology. Folktale has its own orderings, but to move from song to tale would be to push along the path of literary as well as of cosmic history, the path of the increase of entropy. The ballad as it stands is laced rather tightly into the patterns of verse that we have associated with redundancy: meter and rhyme, formulaic phrase, internal repetition of various kinds. In fact the patterned quality of the ballad is even more thoroughgoing than the discipline of these conventions. In defiance of the claim pressed so far in this study that song words are not to be expected to show complex two-dimensional structures, this oral-traditional ballad can be parsed out quite schematically if we treat it as text. The diagrammatic scheme on page 64 illustrates this.

It must be insisted that the ballad is by nature a performance and not a text. But when the text is captured, as the shadow cast into space by the ballad in time, it falls into a startlingly rigorous symmetrical pattern of boxes within boxes. The outside framing pair of stanzas open and close the ballad with colloquies between mother and son, not found in any intervening stanza. The first of these opens with rain and the last ends with trees, the natural setting at the limits of the frame around the human action. Within these stanzas is a frame of warning about the Child's conduct and of punishment consequent on his conduct. Within these is a balanced pair of stanzas moving the action from first scene to second and from second to third; in the former the Child runs to meet three children, and in the latter the three mothers of the children run to meet the Child's mother. Within these is a pair in which insult is paid out by the children to the Child, and then retribution is paid back by the Child to the children. Within these is a single stanza of reversal on which the whole ballad pivots, in the

As it fell out on a Holy day,
  The drops of rain did fall, did fall,
Our Saviour asked leave of His mother Mary
  If he might go play at ball.

"To play at ball, my own dear Son,
  It's time You was going or gone,
But be sure let me hear no complaint of You
  At night when You do come home."

It was upling scorn and downling scorn,
  Oh, there He met three jolly jerdins:
Oh, there He asked the three jolly jerdins
  If they would go play at ball.

"Oh, we are lords' and ladies' sons,
  Born in bower or in hall,
And You are but some poor maid's child
  Born'd in an ox's stall."

"If you are lords' and ladies' sons
  Born'd in bower or in hall,
Then at the very last I'll make it appear
  That I am above you all."

Our Saviour built a bridge with the beams of the sun,
  And over it He gone, He gone He,
And after followed the three jolly jerdins,
  And drownded they were all three.

It was upling scorn and downling scorn
  The mothers of them did whoop and call,
Crying out, "Mary mild, call home your Child,
  For ours are drownded all."

Mary mild, Mary mild, called home her Child,
  And laid our Saviour across her knee,
And with a whole handful of bitter withy
  She gave Him slashes three.

Then He says to His Mother, "Oh, the withy! oh! the withy,
  The bitter withy that causes me to smart, to smart,
Oh! the withy it shall be the very first tree
  That perishes at the heart."

first half of which the Child accepts as proposition the status asserted by the children, and in the second half of which he draws as conclusion an inverted order of status.

Diagrams of traditional ballads similar to this sketch have been constructed by David Buchan, who argues that such patterns are actually the essence of oral narrative verse.

> In addition to . . . sometimes intricate aural patterns of assonance and alliteration, oral poems frequently possess quite complex architectonic patterns. These latter patterns manifest themselves structurally and conceptually, in all kinds of balances and parallelisms, contrasts and antitheses, chiastic and framing devices, and in various kinds of triadic groupings . . . [which] reflect how [the nonliterate person's] mode of apprehension is spatial as well as simply linear and sequential.

> Framing—the annular device or ring composition, as it is known to the Homerists—is one of the hallmarks of oral poetry . . . [by which the maker can] keep a grip on the interrelations of all parts of the poem.[5]

In a genuinely oral, unwritten ballad, such as "The Bitter Withy" is attested to be, we meet a thicket of structures that are not only elusive of our perception in performance but that could not, I think, even be lucidly described without written diagram, or at least the visualization of the written-out script of that performance. To say they are "spatial" is metaphorical, though helpful. The territory of which these patterns are the map is not spatial stuff but temporal process.

That such patterns over time should somehow inhere in the words of the song, put there by the maker and constituent in the listener's experience when neither has text to consult, may seem not unreasonable when we consider that the ballad's music presupposes a similar apprehension of pattern over time, although of somewhat shorter extent, over less time—the length of a stanza. The tune to which the words are set is, like the architectonics, an ordering that works itself out in departure and return, rising and falling tension, opening and closure. It is likewise a pattern to which little conscious attention is given as it measures itself out once per stanza through the song. As musically and otherwise literate, we are able to write spatial analogues for such patterns and then to read them and talk about them. Apart from experience of such writing, they are hard to think about and explain.

The presence of musical pattern makes song, among the various kinds of verbal artifacts, the most distinctively time-patterned form. Even if hidden chiastic or other structures lurk in folktales, for example, the ballad that shares those patterns is higher up on the ladder of ordering patterns over time, because it adds together the short-range patterning common to all versification, the long-range patterning of skillful oral construction, and the intermediate-range patterning of shapely melody. All of these patterns rise above and govern the continuity of which we are most conscious in the ballad, whether hearing or reading. What we see first and most is the narrative logic happening in passing time, what the ballad shares with story. From the perspective that is cognizant of that narrative flow, the large patterns that are being traced out and fulfilled are either shadowy or invisible. Yet in song, more fully than in most verbal constructs, those patterns sustain and constrain the words. In the oral ballad they bind the words more tightly even than considerations of sense do. The discursive continuity of the ballad story may be telescoped in or out by insertion or omission of stanzas; the logical consistency or circumstantial accuracy of the story may be honored or breached; semantic clarity may be muffled by formulaic expression or completely stifled in nonsense words, in a way that puzzles discursive understanding of the linear narrative.

As is true in other kinds of song, conscious attention is not drawn to large structural patterns when ballads are sung. To say that our attention is not catching the time-spanning patterns of the ballad is not to say that they are irrelevant to our experience. On the contrary, such patterns have a deeply formative role in that experience, proportional to their peremptory power over the words they allow to stand in the sequence of the text. "The Bitter

Withy" as song is experienced two ways at once, the way of event-sequence and the way of other-than-sequential order.

The nature of the two kinds of experience may be further described, though not very full explained, by reference to current thinking about human brain function. The two varieties of experience correlate with the work performed by the two nearly symmetrical halves of the human cerebral cortex. Words gathered into musical pattern appear to be the province of different departments of the brain from those that take in, process, and give out other verbal business. The testimony of contemporary medicine is conveniently summarized by Julian Jaynes in his controversial book on the history of consciousness (the use to be made of those facts here does not presuppose Jaynes's own provocative conclusions):

> Speech, as has long been known, is a function primarily of the left cerebral hemisphere. But song, as we are presently discovering, is a function of the right. . . . The evidence is various but consistent.
>
> . . . Patients who have suffered cerebral hemorrhages on the left hemisphere such that they cannot speak can still sing.
>
> . . . When the left hemisphere is sedated . . . the person is unable to speak but can still sing. When the injection is on the right so that only the left hemisphere is active, the person can speak but cannot sing.
>
> . . . One . . . patient with only a speechless right hemisphere to his name was able to sing "America" and "Home on the Range." . . .
>
> Electrical stimulation on the right hemisphere in regions adjacent to the posterior temporal lobe . . . often produces hallucinations of singing and music.[6]

The dependence of singing on right-hemisphere activity sheds light on the nature of songs as marriages of music and words and also on the nature and function of the patterns in addition to music that have been discovered binding oral compositions. Cautions must be made: creation, performance, and apprehension of songs must normally involve the collaborative activity of both halves of the brain; and in any case specialization of function between those halves is not absolute. All distinctions between the cerebral hemispheres seem to admit of qualification and exception. Nevertheless it appears that in general the use of words in prose and in normal speech, on the one hand, and the use of words in songs, on the other, are governed by different areas of the brain and may take place with some independence of each other and by quite different rules.

Consider the recall of a song lodged in memory. It returns intact, and the more easily the less scrutiny we give to its discursive aspect as we produce it. Harold Gordon and Joseph Bogen, who conducted the experiments of anesthetizing one hemisphere and then the other to test production of speech and singing, distinguish two processes of recall for two kinds of verbal material:

> The dichotomy between language and speech, on the one hand, and singing on the other, may be differentiated on a level related to their construction. For example, a sentence, paragraph, phrase, or, in short, speech is composed from several morpheme units which are retrieved from memory according to grammatical rules and are ordered into a specified temporal arrangement. In contrast, songs, melodies, as well as many everyday prosaic passages are remembered and produced as intact wholes. The parts of these units are not pieced together tone by tone, word by word, but rather are recalled all at once as a complete unit. The ability to store and recall intact such large units may be an important aspect of those tasks for which the right hemispheres of most individuals are dominant.[7]

Doctors Gordon and Bogen conclude that this difference of functions may be most generally described with respect to the dimension of time. One set of functions of the brain deals with material that is "time independent—that is, complete units unrelated to others"; the other set, "time dependent—that is, units related to others successively in time. . . . Reliance upon 'time' as a principle of organization may better distinguish the left from the right hemisphere: the left is crucially concerned with it, whereas the right is not."[8]

What is meant by "time-independent" here is more fully explored in another essay by Bogen. He suggests:

> We can say that the right hemisphere has a highly developed "appositional" capacity. This term implies a capacity for apposing or comparing perceptions, schemas, engrams, etc. . . . The rules or methods by which propositional thought is elaborated on "this" [the left] side of the brain (the side which speaks, reads, and writes) have been subjected to analysis of syntax, semantics, mathematical logic, etc., for many years. The rules by which appositional thought is elaborated on the other side of the brain will need study for many years to come.[9]

Two other researchers suggest that the right, "the mute, minor hemisphere is specialized for Gestalt perception, being primarily a synthesist in dealing with information input."[10]

"Time-independent," "appositional," and "Gestalt," as characterizations of the activity of the right hemisphere, the part of the brain on which song primarily depends, indicate that the binding of song words into patterns above the flow of discursive syntax is what distinguishes song and related phenomena from speech, or from prose. Clinical researchers have investigated the tie of words specifically to music, in modern songs in modern brains. It is suggested here that the ballad patternings in addition to tune, the groupings and architecture of stanzas, likewise are the coinage and currency of the right side of the brain, made by and for people not schooled to the linear discipline of writing. Oral culture, where no one is literate, uses highly patterned, formularized speech, relying much more than we do on the "appositional" capacities of mind; or as Buchan has said, such culture evinces that its "mode of apprehension is spatial as well as simply linear and sequential."

Story may verge toward song, depending on the degree of time-independent patterning it shows, but sheer story is in the other camp from story-song: it is left-hemisphere stuff. Brenda Milner has conducted experiments that show this:

> Disturbance in the recall of verbal material, which regularly accompanies lesions of the left temporal lobe when speech is represented in the left hemisphere . . . has been shown both for verbal associative learning . . . and for story recall (Milner, 1958). . . . Patients with left-temporal-lobe epilepsy will recall significantly fewer items from a short prose passage that has been read to them earlier. . . . [Left-temporal lobectomy] patients now reproduce logically connected verbal material in a very fragmented way. [11]

Narrative logic is time-dependent and separate from the organizational modes seated on the right side, where song is accommodated.

Such patterns as the annular or chiastic structures in ballads were no doubt generated by the ballad-makers to some degree separately from the linear calculation and planning we associate with composition; similarly, they were no doubt apprehended by the nonliterate audience in a mode different from the concurrent awareness of the linear sense of the story. Perhaps for them as well as for us there was no acknowledging of bracketing patterns as the song streamed past; but such patterns must have contributed a sense of rightness and good form to which we are now dull. Our songs do without any similar degree of patterning, and besides, they are mostly shorter. The versification and music that define songs for us are two remaining employments of a faculty that in oral culture could deal in much larger spanning patterns; they are still enough to refer song away from the reading and writing left half of the brain.

It was said in the introduction that the experience of song is in some sense static. The present point offers a sense for "static."

The static quality has to do with song having been shaped into musical pattern, and perhaps further patterns, not dependent on time—a fixity, that sounds in time move to fulfill. Time is not change in song experience, for change would break the fixity. Song pattern is an apparent victory over time, a notion that might have intrigued John Keats. Keats noted on this subject that a full experience of beauty can "tease us out of thought/As doth eternity." The awareness of time-independent forms in song may not be present to rational thought; it may instead, if thought is only linear and prosaic, liberate us from thought and time.

Mention of Keats is a reminder of how far the present discussion has drawn song back toward other kinds of poetry. Considered with respect to brain function, song and poetry work much alike. The patterns of ballad discussed here can appear, and work similarly, in written verse. Keats furnishes an excellent example. His literary "ballad," "La Belle Dame Sans Merci," has been shown by Earl Wasserman to have a beautifully symmetrical structure of stanza and character grouping. Wasserman's masterful explication of "Ode on a Grecian Urn" reveals an astonishing array of extended patterns in that poem, some of them annular or chiastic. In diagrams that make horizontal miniatures of the bracket patterns in "The Bitter Withy," Walter Jackson Bate has traced assonantal sound patterns in some of Keats's lines; for example:

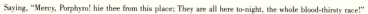
Saying, "Mercy, Porphyro! hie thee from this place; They are all here to-night, the whole blood-thirsty race!"
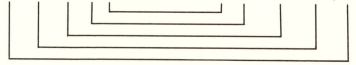

Keats himself talked about the musical patterns possible in verse, and "chanted" sound-patterned verse such as Chatterton's.[12]

The same general kind of thinking, then, can create and perceive time-independent patterns in poetry as well as in song, and indeed in any artful expression through time, in *Tom Jones* or in the *Iliad*.[13] Fiction differs from history, if history itself is not so ordered, by its participation in mythic patterns that assert fixity within flow; and if, as Joseph Campbell argues, the shape of all narrative is departure and return, perhaps all fiction is even chiastic, coming back past its markers in the reverse order of the way it met them first.

Our example of orally composed narrative song has shown in a pure form the confrontation of the artist with time, and his (not necessarily conscious) recourse to certain patterns to fence and build his performance as an intact, well-formed thing. Without the fixity of "text," he envisions and elaborates a pattern so highly redundant in its government of words that it does not matter much what his actual words are—they will vary with his next singing of the song, until the age of literacy. Then the words come to be regarded as part of the fixity and to be stored away in right-hemisphere memory, locked together into large units especially by their accompanying melody pattern.

In the literate age song and written poetry divide between them the domain inherited from preliterate bards. Given the new assumption that text is fixed, poetry fills in its time-independent large patterns with increasingly time-dependent, sequential, uniquely worded lines; it asks its reader to follow the developing sense of what it says from line to line to the end. Song remains much more committed to its time-independent patterns, pulled back by the influence of its music. Now that it is memorized as set text rather than grasped as narrative pattern, it moves away from formula but is unable to pursue the communicative continuity of time-dependent speech very far. It must choose words that will work in the appositional perception its music invokes. Its lines must participate in the whole rather than lead step by step to the conclusion.

It may be noted, finally, that in this evolution of the appearance of fixed written text, narrative song is on the whole replaced by lyric song; the more literate a society, the fuller the replacement. A logic suggests itself here. With literacy, the overarching structures of oral narrative are no longer necessary to specify what will be said when; and as they are no longer relied on they become less available. The songwriter loses the challenge that faced the oral poet of managing time with his mind alone. Relying on the crutch of a text, he gives up the craft of patterning a story. Narrative can be planned out on paper now in prose or poetry. But in song the time-independent patterns of the music pull the mind away from linear continuity, and failing the old readiness to produce or apprehend the larger patterns through many stanzas, the songwriter moves toward the voicing of one moment's state of feeling that is lyric.

Art Song: "I care not for these Ladies"

I care not for these Ladies
That must be woode and praide,
Give me kind Amarillis
The wanton countrey maide;
Nature art disdaineth,
Her beautie is her owne;
     Her when we court and kisse,
     She cries, forsooth, let go:
     But when we come where comfort is,
     She never will say no.

If I love Amarillis,
She gives me fruit and flowers,
But if we love these Ladies,
We must give golden showers;
Give them gold that sell love,
Give me the Nutbrowne lasse,
     Who when we court and kisse,
     She cries, forsooth, let go:
     But when we come where comfort is,
     She never will say no.

These Ladies must have pillowes,
And beds by strangers wrought,
Give me a Bower of willowes,
Of mosse and leaves unbought,
And fresh Amarillis,
With milke and honie fed,
     Who when we court and kisse,
     She cries, forsooth, let go:
     But when we come where comfort is,
     She never will say no.

THOMAS CAMPION published this song among twenty-one pieces comprising the first half of *A Booke of Ayres* in 1601. The book carried on its title page the name of his friend the lutenist Philip Rosseter, but inside it avowed that Campion had written the words and music of these songs in the first half. Campion was already known at the time as a writer of Latin verse and of English songs; his first efforts had appeared ten years earlier at about the time London first saw plays by Shakespeare. Rosseter and Campion's book is an early landmark in a brief period, a quarter of a century between 1597 and 1622, which is the golden age of sophisticated English song. These are the dates of publication of the lute songbooks, containing songs for solo voice and lute accompaniment (with the option of other performance arrangements). Together with a slightly earlier but overlapping vogue for madrigal, which interweaves several voices and gives interest to music over words, this period represents a special time of convergence, in which the best composers set lyric verse written by the first rank of their contemporary poets, including Sidney, Spenser, and Jonson, and even a playful bit of Shakespeare and, somewhat overboldly, a few poems by Donne. Campion is the best of the handful of these writers who created both verse and music, sophisticated verse artfully set to artful music.[1]

"I care not for these Ladies" is both pastoral and courtly, in a wry combination. (The anticourtly was one established mode of the courtly.) By Campion's time, the tradition of courtly love lyrics, a fancy throughout aristocratic Europe during the high middle ages, was disappearing. Its English phase had flourished from Chaucer to Wyatt and on into the work of the lesser Elizabethans.[2] Sidney, Spenser, and Shakespeare use the forms of the old courtly game for new poetical ends and transcend the avocational courtesy verse of their predecessors. In the seventeenth century, the poets of the schools of Donne and Jonson, and even the cavalier dandies, are no longer mistakable for courtly lovers. But at the end of the sixteenth century the clichés of courtly love could still be put together into pastiches little changed from those two hundred years earlier, as may be seen among the airs in this same book that were set and possibly also written by Rosseter:

If she forsake me, I must die:
   Shall I tell her so?
Alas, then strait she will reply
   No, no, no, no, no.
If I disclose my desp'rate state
She will but make sport thereat
   And more unrelenting grow.
                [XVII]

Something much more lively than this is happening in most of Campion's lyrics. Ralph Berringer distinguishes such verse from what Campion wrote: in most of Campion's lyrics as in "I care not for these Ladies," "there is little talk of vows and endless love and unrequited service. . . . At least seven lyrics of Part I celebrate physical embraces."[3] Something more lively again, more intense, is happening in the contemporary lyrics of Donne. Rosseter's as well as much Tudor versification is made easily into unassuming song verse. Its highly redundant conventional vocabulary, its stock notions and situations, and its urbane impersonalness mated naturally, with few demands, to any tune of the proper cut. Donne's verse on the other hand is mostly unsingable. Campion's words, between these two poles, challenge and reward careful setting. One way to describe his significance is to say that in a history of increasing complexity, immediacy, and personalness in the English lyric, Campion's verses represent the latest stage before what seems interesting in lyric is too complex to set. This question will be considered again at the end of the chapter.

We will be examining in this chapter various kinds of complexity and discriminating those distinctive of artful song from those that are bad for musical setting. Among lyrics by Thomas Campion, "I care not for these Ladies" is perhaps not the most subtle in its line of thought. Campion is now argued to be more complicated than he was formerly thought to be. John T. Irwin has sought in a suggestive study to show that Campion has "a balanced, multi-level meaning" such that he "can compete on the highest poetic level," and Irwin displays this complexity in Campion's song beginning "Now winter nights enlarge."[4] The kinds of complexity Irwin shows there we will also see in the present song, but there is a difference between the two songs that we should pause to notice. Here is the text of that other lyric:

Now winter nights enlarge
  The number of their houres
And clouds their stormes discharge
  Upon the ayrie towres;
Let now the chimneys blaze
  And cups o'erflow with wine,
Let well-tun'd words amaze
  With harmonie divine.
Now yellow waxen lights
  Shall waite on hunny Love,
While youthfull Revels, Masks, and Courtly sights,
  Sleepes leaden spels remove.

This time doth well dispence
  With lovers long discourse;
Much speech hath some defence,
  Though beauty no remorse.
All doe not all things well:
  Some measures comely tread,
Some knotted Ridles tell,
  Some Poems smoothly read.

The Summer hath his joyes,
  And Winter his delights;
Though Love and all his pleasures are but toyes,
  They shorten tedious nights.

Though, to borrow Donne's line, the reader who has read these verses cursorily has not Donne, he has not quite done with understanding them either. As Irwin argues, these lines are not metaphysical, and yet they are complicated and contain turns that may be missed, even if the modern reader is helped over the artificial obstacle posed by the fact that *dispence with* in the first lines of the second stanza meant the opposite then from what it does now. The third and fourth lines of the second stanza are not as clear an antithesis as we first think. We may slip again at "All doe not all things well," which by itself has a negativity that evaporates as activities are listed: the emerging point is diversity and the divergence of what is appropriate at different seasons. (The line translates Virgil's *Non omnia possumus omnes*, which Campion apparently liked; he quoted it in the preface to his later *Two Bookes of Ayres*. It must have had special piquancy to a man who wrote, and wrote about, both music and poetry and who studied law and practiced medicine.) A lyric that has these turns, or at least a lyric that had even a few more of them, would be straining the limits of song. Campion's verse at times edges near the limit. In pursuit of a distinction between singable and unsingable complexities, we may begin with this: the "balanced, multi-level meaning" that Irwin finds in this second lyric is good for making a subtle song to the extent that the various layers of meaning tend in the same direction, reinforcing and validating each other. To the extent that its complexity makes kinks in our reading, making us look back and revise what we thought we had caught, it is not good for song. In these terms the second stanza of "Now winter nights enlarge" has two potential flaws in its text as text for song, which Campion's music may or may not redeem. His sophistication is daring and often triumphant, exploring the whole range of what works easily, what works miraculously, and what does not

quite work. Where "Now winter nights enlarge" is a more competitive Jacobean lyric, "I care not for these Ladies," which is less
tortuous, is more finished song. Still, this flippant lyric has considerable artful complexity.

The compressed spring that stores the energy of this mock-
simple lyric is the double negative of resistance resisted. It begins by rejecting ladies who reject and ends by embracing the lass
who does not say no. In one of his essays E. H. Gombrich remarks that the essence of sophisticated taste is denial: we become
sophisticated when we deny ourselves simple gratifications. A
typical refinement of sophistication, then, present, for example,
in anything pastoral, is the turning of sophistication against itself
and affirming what is asserted to be simple, from the position of
having experienced and rejected what is refined. There are more
and less serious modes of this rejection of sophistication. There
can be a profound sense of renewal in passing beyond fastidious-
ness to a new grasp of the essential, as when Beethoven creates
song at the climax of his final symphony. Campion's poem is only a
small and cheery gesture of turning back to the basic, although its
kinship with the grand eternal return cannot be completely forgotten. Certainly there is a real urge expressed in these words. Campion certainly felt it, as most people feel it. On the other hand the
song certainly remains a city and a courtly song while it praises
the country girl; it is a song for city and courtly people. Like the
young poet Yeats declaring "I will arise and go now" to a rural
island retreat, the singer who sings this to his lute is staying
where he is. The song fits the courtly game, as a tease and exhor-
tation to present ladies and as a male boast.

Campion's most recent editor, Walter R. Davis, notes that "the
rustic quality of the song is stressed by the meter (in part, the old-
fashioned 'poulter's measure' of the 1560s and '70s) and the music, for it is set to a country dance tune, a jig."[5] The versification
and the dancing rhythm of the music mirror the tone of the text,
sophisticated art dressed out as simple. The portion of the lyric in
poulter's measure is the refrain (measured as the poulterer sells
eggs, fourteen syllables in the second dozen), a device common in

folk song that Campion does not use in any other air; elsewhere he makes use only occasionally of one- and two-line burdens. The refrain is cleverly annexed to the stanza so as to extend and complete it, besides standing self-contained as the character of Amarillis in the clinch. (The music is marked to repeat the refrain whole, so that the refrain finishes each stanza subordinated to and completing it, and then each time also stands up alone.) The whole stanza, including the refrain, has the form of, first, a quatrain, alternately rhyming—with alternately masculine and feminine rhymes; then the first two lines of another such quatrain, like the opening lines except for the dropping of an unstressed syllable; and then, instead of the closing of a second quatrain, two lines with other final sounds, and then two lines completing *those* two lines to resolve a second, postponed quatrain. The postponement is in the two lines where Amarillis's compliance hangs in the balance, a line of courting, a line of resisting—and then comes the overbearing line of pressing beyond her resistance, pushing ahead with an extra metrical unit and no rest into the final line of nonresistance and gratification.

In another essay Davis writes of Campion's work that "his songbooks abound in lyrics whose settings reinforce subdivisions by melodic changes and indicate the relations between subdivisions by melodic relationships."[6] Such melodic mirroring of the poem is visible in "I care not for these Ladies," the jigging music reflecting the metrics that reflect what the verses say in general, and the components of the tune suiting closely to the parts of the lyric that they set. The first line of the music sets the first two verses of each stanza, the first half of the quatrain, describing either Amarillis or the ladies; it is repeated for the second two verses, describing the other. The line consists of two consecutive bouncy phrases. The next line, for the next pair of verses, the odd pair, begins a third below and ends perched a third above the tonic, away from the resolution but not in the dominant chord that anticipates immediate return. Instead comes the brief drama of the courting of Amarillis. The melody steps back and starts where the previous half-line started, and in a new dotted rhythm flirts

toward the tonic and away but less far, away and back to a distance of only one tone. Then the final line of music, where the
words assert masculine overriding of this token opposition, hits
that tone twice with firm stresses and reaches through to the tonic
base (on "comfort"). It steps away, and the dancing dotted rhythm
sets one more quick, smooth, symmetrical curve (to "never" a
fifth away) and back (to "no"), the double negative that means
yes.

When Irwin argues that Campion's lyrics show complexity, he
constructs an impressive analysis of the phonemic patterning in
"Now winter nights enlarge." Patterning of the sounds of words is
likewise visible in "I care not for these Ladies." Before we em-
bark on analysis of these patterns, however, two cautions must be
admitted, both having to do with the question of how significant a
given level of patterning may be. Some sound patterning is common to the generality of lyric poetry: "Where lyrical feeling or
sensuous description occurs in European poetry, there will usually be found patterns of vowels and consonants."[7] We have seen
in the introduction that it may often be prominent in song verse
in particular. Further, some such patterning is discoverable in
very ordinary language use, as Stephen Booth observes (Booth's
emphases):

> *In*significant and/or un*in*tentional verbal effects figure largely
> *in* casual conversation and *in* good and bad workaday prose;
> they trigger our *in*stinct for making and hearing puns, and
> they are often the unsought key by which we know when a par-
> agraph addressed to the gas company is or is not as we want
> it.[8]

Analysis of sound patterns, then, while it can certainly illuminate
the small causes of our sense of rightness in good verse (or prose),
is difficult to use for proving that some lyric is complex and artful
in an absolute sense, as Irwin comes close to doing. There is, in
Edward Sapir's phrase, "chance as the ever-present rival con-
jecture," and there is the uncalculated level of what is ordinary in
verse.[9]

III.

I care not for these Ladies that must be wooed and praide,
Giue me kind Amarillis the wanton countrey maide,
Nature art disdaineth, her beautie is her owne, Her when we court & kisse, she cries forsooth let go, but
when we come where comfort is she neuer will say no.

If I loue Amarillis,
She giues me fruit and flowers,
But if we loue these Ladies,
We must giue golden showers,
Giue them go'd that sell loue,
Giue me the Nutbrowne lasse,
    VVho when we court, &c.

These Ladies must haue pillowes,
And beds by strangers wrought,
Giue me a Bower of willowes,
Of mosse and leaues vnbought,
And fresh Amarillis
With milke and honie fed,
    VVho when we court, &c.

"I care not for these ladies," by Thomas Campion. From Philip Rosseter, *A Booke of Ayres*, 1601.

Sobered by these warnings, we may consider some of the ways sounds dance in the consort of these specific verses.

I care not for these Ladies	*1*
That must be woode and praide,	*2*
Give me kind Amarillis	*3*
The wanton countrey maide;	*4*
Nature art disdaineth,	*5*
Her beautie is her owne;	*6*
Her when we court and kisse,	*7*
She cries, forsooth, let go:	*8*
But when we come where comfort is,	*9*
She never will say no.	*10*

Davis remarks that the alliteration on /k/ reinforces the Elizabethan sexual joke in "countrey" maid, and Irwin adds that the assonant words in line 9 are likewise capable of sexual innuendo. (Parallel cases may be enjoyed in Eric Partridge's *Shakespeare's Bawdy*.) Note that the alliterating words include all the verbs of *I* and *we* (*care*, *court*, *kisse*, and *come*) and Amarillis's verb of struggle (*cries*) and that all of these words fall under metrical stress. *Kind* is an important thematic word (see below), but it misses stress and lacks parallel or antithetical alliterated adjectival companions and probably should be conceded to chance.

The matter of assonance and alliteration may be pursued further. Dell Hymes has investigated a series of sonnets by Wordsworth and Keats in search of instances where some important word that is crucial to the meaning of the poem also gathers the sonnet's "particular aggregate of sound."[10] Something of the sort happens here with *countrey*, presumably the most interesting word in the stanza. Its constituent phonemes are distributed throughout the lines of this stanza: (1) KRNTRE, (2) TENR, (3) EKNR, (4) NNKNTRE, (5) NTRRTN, (6) RTERN, (7) RNEK-RTNK, (8) EKRT, (9) TNEKRKRT, (10) ENRN; or if we sort and subtract, KNTRE, NTRE, KNRE, KNTRE, NTR, NTRE, KN-TRE, KTRE, KNTRE, NRE. The /k/ sound appears only one other time in all the other twelve lines of verse in the poem. The

number of different members of this sound group to appear in
each of those other lines is about 2.4, while here it is about 4.2
per line. Echoes of the related *come* are present but more sparse
in these same lines: (1) K, (2) M, (3) MKM, (4) KM, (7) KK, (8)
K, (9) KMKM.

The same question asked of the whole lyric shows that the
sounds of the name *Amarillis* ring back and forth in every line. It
is hard to say how many of these common consonants would appear in every random grouping of a few words, but there does
seem to be consistent echoing of them here. Counting voiced and
voiceless sibilants /s/ and /z/, and both nasals /m/ and /n/, we can
show the following, before and after rearranging:

	I		II		III
(1) RNRZLZ	: NRLZ	(11) LMRLS	: MRLS	(21) ZLZMSLZ	: M LS
(2) MSR	: MR S	(12) MRNLRZ	: MRLZ	(22) NZSRNRZR	: NR S
(3) MMRLS	: MRLS	(13) LZLZ	: LZ	(23) MRLZ	: MRLZ
(4) NNRM	: NR	(14) MSLNRZ	: MRLS	(24) MSNLZN	: M LS
(5) NRRSN	: NR S	(15) MLSLL	: M LS	(25) NRMRLS	: MRLS
(6) RZRN	: NR Z	(16) MNRLS	: MRLS	(26) MLNN	: M L
	—		—		—
(7) RNRNS	: NR S				
(8) RZRSL	: RLS		[refrain]		[refrain]
(9) NMRMRZ	: MR Z				
(10) NRLSN	: NRLS				

Probably it would be no less informative just to say that lines like
"She gives me fruit and flowers" or "Give me a Bower of willowes"
whisper "Amarillis" behind their other words.

A few other patterns may be noted in the second and third
stanzas.

If I love Amarillis,	*11*
She gives me fruit and flowers,	*12*
But if we love these Ladies,	*13*
We must give golden showers;	*14*
Give them gold that sell love,	*15*
Give me the Nutbrowne lasse . . .	*16*

seem to be ruled by *love* and *give*. The sounds /f/, /v/, and /l/ run
through the stanza very consistently: (11) FLVL, (12) VFFL, (13)
FLVL, (14) VL, (15) VLLV, (16) VL. Groupings of /g/ and /f/, /v/
are about equally dense: (11) V, (12) GV, (13) V, (14) GV, (15)
GVGV, (16) GV.

These Ladies must have pillowes,	21
And ḇeds by strangers wrought,	22
Give me a Ḇower of willowes,	23
Of mosse and leaves unḇought,	24
And fresh Amarillis,	25
With milke and honie fed . . .	26

shows a procession of initial *b*'s in (22), (23), (24), on the first,
second, and third stresses respectively. A subset of the phonemes
of *Amarillis* emerges in *milk* in the last line, which seems to be
steadily anticipated in the preceding lines: (21) *LMḺ*, (23) *MḺ*,
(24) *MḺ*, (25) *MḺ*, (26) *MḺ* (emphasis when initial consonants of
stressed syllables). This unobtrusive place in the analysis may be
best for a brief excursus on this "milk" in the substance and sub-
substance of the lyric. Amarillis is associated verbally with fruit,
nut, milk, honey, and being fed; in the third stanza she is served
up fresh on a bed of moss and leaves; the actions of the courting of
her are kissing and crying. The fantasy appears to have an oral
bias, not surprising perhaps in a highly articulated construct for
singing. We may guess that, in a byway of the imagining of this
lyric, the anatomical place where comfort is is the breast.

The sense and the imagery of the lyric remain to be considered at large. Much of what has been said so far has assumed the
obvious distinction that is the basis of the lyric—between Amarillis and these ladies. As this is cultivated song, we have said,
the poles of the opposition are not exactly court and country, but
court and its imaginary antitype. Around the poles cluster the attributes of civilization and artifice on the one hand, and of something called "Nature" on the other. ("Nature" is one of the two
complexions of the word "kind" applied to the heroine. "Kind"
had in Campion's time two senses predominating over our usage

that associates the word to patronizing solicitude in general, as toward animals. One of these was courtly jargon: of a mistress, "disposed to condescend to comply"; the other was "manifesting Nature or what is right and natural," as in Hamlet's judgment on marriage tainted with incest, "a little more than kin and less than kind.") For present purposes it will suffice to notice that this Nature is imagined by negation of what exists or is pretended to exist in the court culture rather than, say, by the most superficial glance at English farm life. The salient fact about the moss and leaves is that they are *unbought*, a negation of social fact rather than an image of something green, soft, damp, or whatever. They are the postulated (not recalled, not imaged) opposite of what one lies down on in London.

The catalogue of the attributes of urban and courtly life that are distinguished by these contrasts is suggestive not so much of the discontents of Campion's time and class, what they might wistfully imagine was lost to them, as of what the culture noticed about itself, how it saw itself developed away from earlier and other possibilities. To describe these aspects of the imagery is also to suggest a miniature self-portrait of the people whose song it is. One fact about Elizabethan high society that is reflected in the pastoral antimirror, for example, is that their ladies must be dealt with verbally, as opposed to manually. This is an enduring caste distinction. Late in the next century Goldsmith pokes fun at a mentality like that of this song in his play *She Stoops to Conquer*, where young Marlow falters in talk with polite women but operates at ease with their social inferiors; when he is maneuvered into treating the former like the latter, the girl's father demands of her, "Didn't I see him haul you about like a milkmaid?" The song takes inverted notice of courtliness as verbal game, where direct handling (called, ironically, "courting") is refined into wooing and praying. It is a verbally polite society, accomplished in talk and likewise in poetry, with pride of place (implies the poet) for such people as poets; probably they are the most successful wooers and prayers. To put it another way, Campion, with great verbal skill, ironically deprecates trafficking in words. One

implication is that this courtier could easily talk around the ladies; he just does not care to do it. Donne employs a similar boast
overtly in "Womans Constancy." Anticipating further comparison
of Campion and Donne below, we should notice that Donne makes
the irony a dramatic surprise in his final lines:

[Will you say this, or this . . . ?]
. . . against these scapes I could
  Dispute, and conquer, if I would
  Which I abstaine to doe,
For by to morrow, I may think so too.

In Campion, by contrast, the verbal antiverbalism falls in with the
thoroughgoing sophisticated antisophistication present from first
to last in this lyric, a resonance of standing pattern as opposed to
a dynamic shift of what is happening as in "Womans Constancy."

"Nature" of the kind called up in the lyric is defined against
art, which is cosmetic: "Nature art disdaineth / Her beautie is
her owne." Art as an attribute of life with the ladies, as part of the
self-perception of their circle, reflects beautifying amenities, the
command of decoration, dresses and surfaces from which to borrow beauty. Beauty is transferable and accessible to all and hence
duplicitous. But the complaint is a disguised self-compliment for
the courtly, that they are all beautiful people to appearance. One
reason the ladies may need to borrow beauty is that they may not
be very fresh, since they are alleged to sell their love. An attribute of sophisticated culture is thus the possibility of preserving
desirable youth when one is no longer a maid. The country girl
who is "wanton" will have a short tenure as maid and will need to
be replaced by a fresh Amarillis; courtly life possesses the sophistication to enjoy and enjoy again and so has partial command
over and exemption from the processes of nature.

Amarillis gives fruit and flowers, where the ladies take money.
Thus distinguished, she is undemanding where they demand;
they are selfish, and she is not spoiled by selfishness. The women
want to provide for their wants, which may or may not be greedy:
it would be rash to judge and not hard to defend them. Amarillis

is unconcerned and free of anxiety for the future, exactly as free
as her pursuer is of anxiety about her future. In fact she has no
future, only freshness in the present, and as such stands as a distinctively suitable fantasy figure for song. The distinction, then,
is not just between whorish corruption and naive generosity.
Amarillis is immediacy. She is singular, unlike the ladies who
come and go, and their plural admirers ("we": there is slight ambiguity about how many admirers Amarillis has, sometimes "I"
and sometimes "we," though "we" who court and kiss and come to
comfort may be Amarillis and I). She is always available and accommodating, unlike ladies who may be preoccupied with things
or men not present. Their partial command over time and processes preoccupies them with what is past and passing and to
come.

At its root the whole opposition is really between the more or
less real world of experience and an imagination of innocence. In
comments on another of Campion's lyrics, "There is a Garden in
her face," John Hollander remarks that the word "flow" is a biblical echo:

There is a Garden in her face,
Where Roses and white Lillies grow;
A heav'nly paradice is that place,
Wherein all pleasant fruits doe flow.

The reference is to "flowing with milk and honey," and in that
lyric "the courtly compliment now turns out to be central moral
vision: the only . . . Earthly Paradise is to be found in beautiful
sexual attainment."[11] Amarillis's diet of milk and honey associates her with the promised paradise in the same way. (Erik Erik-
son argues a general connection between the ideal of Eden and
the oral stage of psychosexual development: "This stage seems to
introduce into psychic life . . . universal nostalgia for a paradise
forfeited."[12]) Her realm of timeless gratification shows by contra-
distinction what life the ladies of this earth and their lovers must
live, contending with the nuisances of time. The same elements

are present that go to make Marvell's great poem "To his Coy Mistress."

An interesting indictment of the ladies in this world is that they demand to have pillows and beds wrought by strangers. This is perhaps anticommercial, but it makes little sense as a complaint against trade, or not enough sense. In the inverting mirror, it does show prosperous commerce. The complaint is not really against buying and selling, or against the specialization of labor. This much specialization—having furniture made—obviously goes back a long way in social history. The complaint is against artifacts needing to be wrought at all. Folktales of original paradise and fall commonly imagine the state of happiness as one not needing arts and crafts: "They did not need to work . . . all things came to them without effort on their part"; later, after loss of innocence, "God . . . taught them the art of forging weapons and tools." (Compare entries from the *Motif-Index of Folk Literature*: A 1346, "Man to earn bread by the sweat of his brow"; A 1346.2, "Man must labor for a living; at first everything too easy"; A 1346.2.1, "Cotton at first already spun into threads"; A 1346.2.2, "Canoes at one time self-propelling.")[13] The attribute of society is that its approach to comfort is impedimenta, a world of work and wealth, a world rich in providing services and making goods. As this is a society that contrives and prepares, it is again showing its dimension of time and process; in the paradise of Amarillis the mossy bed is eternally ready, with no past, neither bought nor made.

One sort of goods made in this world, in late Renaissance English society, is songs. Songs of Campion's sort are wrought by strangers and bought from booksellers. They can be wrought, like this one, with much art, which is best when concealed. There is a mystique of the easy art of a leisured courtier; there is a sentimental idealization of what is simple and artless; there is a notion that art as well as sex is most nearly perfect when it comes to us without contrivance. The mock-simplicity and skillfully concealed artifice of "I care not for these Ladies" picture themselves in the

vignette of Amarillis's bower where the bed, as Keats said was
true of good poetry, comes as naturally as the leaves on the trees.

It may be useful now to ask what difference it makes if this
whole explication of the imagery in the lyric should fail to be persuasive to the reader of independent mind. It might well be denied that some of these resonances are present, just as it might be
denied that the phonemic patterning is significant in the whole or
in parts, or that the music significantly cooperates with the words
in the programmatic way outlined above. Is it likely, since the
song is surely complex, that disagreements will lead to widely di-
vergent ideas of what it is all about? If one selection and emphasis
rather than another among such comments as those assembled
here should be preferred, will the meaning taken be significantly
different?

I do not think that readings of "I care not for these Ladies"
will be very different from each other, whether readers judge this
explication to be excessive or partial, or, given reasonably frequent concurrence, whether they would replace parts of it. This
prediction of consensus is more subject to disproof than to proof,
but it is founded on what I take to be the nature of this lyric.
When Irwin explicates "Now winter nights enlarge," he finds multiple levels of meaning, and he finds also that they are mutually
supporting:

> It is significant that the last two lines of the first stanza are
> capable of meaning on three different levels at once. . . . In
> their ability to mean on three levels simultaneously . . . [they]
> are like a cadential chord which forms a temporary meeting
> point for three themes. . . . This harmonic structure also op-
> erates in the last two lines of the second stanza.[14]

The point is that although the lyric he studies is "as complex a
short poem as one could wish" (Irwin is aware of the way an ap-
petite for complexity reflects the taste of the makers of explica-
tions), the multiplicity of elements in the poem is convergent. Patterns reinforce each other. Convergence is what is claimed here

for the multiple layers of pattern that have been adduced in "I care not for these Ladies." Phonemic patterning may or may not be significant, but if it is, its obvious elements support the main line of what happens in the song, as the elements of the musical arrangement support the melody line of that music—and also as that music, to the extent it interacts with the text, acts to emphasize the patterns of the text. With or without various elements of the complex substructure argued here, the simply balanced configuration of the lyric remains stable. We are neither puzzled nor misled by what we first see or hear in it. And, although absence of proof is not proof of absence, although disturbing elements cannot be proven absent because they have not been brought forward, the equanimity of "I care not for these Ladies" is unlikely to be disturbed by other analyses when this much of this analysis converges.

Campion's lyrics are harmoniously complex. There are other kinds of complexity. Since Eliot praised the metaphysical poets in 1921, the example of Donne has helped English and American students of poetry admire a different kind of complexity. Eliot found the metaphysicals proper models for a modern age:

> Our civilization comprehends great variety and complexity, and this variety and complexity, playing upon a refined sensibility, must produce various and complex results. The poet must become more and more comprehensive, more allusive, more indirect.

When he praises Donne's brilliant image of "A bracelet of bright hair about the bone," he sees in it a "sudden contrast of association," a "telescoping of images and multiplied associations."[15] Metaphysical poetry, beginning contemporary with Campion, asks different and more active participation from its readers than do the airs, and it is not very willing to be sung. R. W. Ingram has written:

> The formal, decorative, impersonal Elizabethan poetry is replaced by the involved and angular, personal, metaphysical

poetry. . . . Simplicity and confidence are replaced by complexity and questioning. Seen in this light Elizabethan poetry
is as happily suitable for music as metaphysical poetry is
not.[16]

The wide-ranging, far-fetched comparisons of the school of Donne
work with "contrast of associations," surprise, drama, the "subtle
sequences of thought or feeling" that John Stevens finds almost
universally absent in the earlier singable Tudor lyric.[17]

It is not only the metaphysical school that diverged from Campion's sort of lyric and the line of musically adaptable verse that
his work crowns. Stephen Booth, in his study and his edition of
Shakespeare's sonnets, has shown how different the complexity of
those sonnets is from the complexity we have seen in the air. The
sonnets display multiple patterns that do not reinforce each other.
There is an "opposition of logical patterns to syntactical patterns
and of both to the metrical pattern and to the rhyme scheme," patterns that run "simultaneously but not concurrently." The sonnets
are rich in "multitudinous meanings, overtones, and suggestions
of reference that are relevant to their context but not necessarily
compatible with each other."[18]

The emergence at about Campion's time of these new kinds of
writing is an epoch in literary history, and in what we may call the
history of literacy within literature. In the long view verbal art
passes from the oral to the written and perhaps on to other things.
The coming of literacy is not a sudden or simple event nor a matter of clear stages. Even when written literary art has a long history of cultivation, as it had already in the sixteenth century, the
transition of poetry and of writing in general from something aiming essentially toward oral presentation to something aiming essentially toward silent, solitary reading is still a matter of evolution. A significant change takes place about 1600. Writers had
long written to be read silently and solitarily as well as, or even
instead of, aloud. About 1600, however, it becomes clear that
writers are exploring the possibilities of being read not only pri-
vately but haltingly—with exploratory curiosity. Shakespeare's

sonnets and Donne's songs and sonnets are poetry of the double-take. They have more to say and do than a single linear course through them can exhaust, and it is from their achievements that we inherit through subsequent ages of poetry our idea of what a lyric poem is.

The change reflected in this beginning of the exclusively literary lyric is not confined to lyric. In the past decade there has come into being a useful and influential critical approach in which Booth's work with the sonnets participates. This approach, associated prominently with the work of Stanley Fish, has argued for analysis of the reader's experience of literature as it unfolds in time. In his book *Self-Consuming Artifacts: the Experience of Seventeenth Century Literature*, Fish reprints his essay "Affective Stylistics" in which he shows the possibility of such observations as that a given sentence "give[s] the reader something and then take[s] it away, drawing him on with the unredeemed promise of its return."[19] Similarly, Booth says that in the sonnets

> a word or phrase can be incomprehensible at the moment it is read and then be effectively glossed by the lines that follow it; a word or phrase can . . . have one meaning as a reader comes to it, another as its sentence concludes, and a third when considered from the vantage point of a summary couplet.

> Sometimes a line signals a syntactic action that later dissolves. . . . Sometimes the syntax sends a reader on abortive side trips.[20]

On the method of such analysis of such literature, Fish writes, "What the method does is *slow down* the reading experience so that 'events' one does not notice in normal time, but which do occur, are brought before our analytical attentions."[21] The track that is traced in this slow-motion study is interesting enough to bother with only because it is not a straight line or a smooth curve but the changing story of scrambling effort to get meaning out of writing.

Although Fish leaves open the question of to what extent his method is applicable to literature of other periods, it is significant that he develops it with respect to seventeenth-century literature, including also in his earlier book on Milton. That age is the time of the flourishing, if perhaps not the birth, of literature for brooding, gradual comprehension and appreciation. The emergence of this standard for literary literacy, the demand for exploratory, broken reading and rereading, by artists in forms that had earlier held themselves available for oral rendition (recall "Some Poems smoothly read" in Campion's winter evening vignette) or equivalently undemanding silent reading, augured among other things the end of the singing of Poetry. Song henceforward is generally conceded to be lighter than real poetry, and since that time poetry set to music has often been poor poetry, or if good poetry it has presented less than its whole self when sung. If it has sometimes been good poetry and worked well with music, that is because it has special virtues that it shares with Campion's airs: unity, convergence of its artful structures, sometimes more of mood or sentiment than we find in "I care not for these Ladies" but rarely more of craft.

Broadside: "Description of a Strange Fish"

𝕬 description of a strange (and miraculous) 𝕱ish, cast upon the sands in the meads, in the 𝕳undred of *Worwell*, in the 𝕮ounty 𝕻alatine of *Chester*, (or *Chesshiere*. 𝕿he certainty whereof is here related concerning the said most monstrous 𝕱ish.

To the tune of *Bragandary*.

Of many maruels in my time
    I'ue heretofore,
But here's a stranger now in prime
    that's lately come on shore,
Inuites my pen to specifie
What some (I doubt) will think a lie.
    O rare
    beyond compare,
  in England nere the like.

The title and the illustration for the broadside are reproduced by permission, from *A Pepysian Garland*, ed. Hyder E. Rollins (Cambridge, Mass.: Harvard University Press, 1971), p. 438.

It is a fish, a monstrous fish,
 a fish that many dreads,
But now it is as we would wish,
 cast vp o'th sands i'th meads,
In Chesshire; *and tis certaine true,*
Describ'd by those who did it view.
 O rare
 beyond compare,
 in England nere the like.

Full twenty one yards and one foot
 this fish extends in length,
With all things correspondent too't,
 for amplitude and strength:
Good people what I shall report,
Doe not account it fained sport.
 O rare
 beyond compare,
 in England nere the like.

It is almost fiue yards in height,
 which is a wondrous thing,
O mark what maruels to our sight
 our Potent Lord can bring.
These secrets Neptune *closely keeps*
Within the bosome of the deeps.
 O rare
 beyond compare,
 in England nere the like.

His lower jaw-bone's fiue yards long,
 the vpper thrice so much,
Twelue yoak of oxen stout and strong,
 (the weight of it is such)
Could not once stir it out o'th sands
Thus works the All-creating hands.

O rare
beyond compare,
in England nere the like.

Some haue a project now in hand,
(which is a tedious taske)
When the Sea turnes, to bring to Land
the same with empty cask:
But how I cannot well conceiue,
To each mans judgment that I leaue.
O rare
beyond compare,
in England nere the like.

The lower jaw-bone nam'd of late,
had teeth in't thirty foure,
Whereof some of them are in weight
two pounds, or rather more:
There were no teeth i'th vpper jaw,
But holes, which many people saw.
O rare
beyond compare,
in England nere the like.

THE SECOND PART, TO THE SAME TUNE.

His Pissle is in length foure yards,
big as a man i'th wast,
This monster he who well regards,
from th' first vnto the last,
By euery part may motiues find,
To wonder at this wondrous kind.
O rare
beyond compare,
in England nere the like.

His Cods are like two hogsheads great,
    this seemeth past beleefe,
But men of credit can relate
    what I describe in briefe:
Then let's with charity confesse
Gods works are more then man can guesse.
    O rare, &c.

The tongue on't is so mighty large,
    I will it not expresse,
Lest I your credit ouer-charge,
    but you may easily guesse,
That sith his shape so far excels,
The tongue doth answer all parts else.
    O rare, &c.

A man on horseback as tis try'd
    may stand within his mouth,
Let none that hears it this deride,
    for tis confirm'd for truth:
By those who dare auouch the same,
Then let the Writer beare no blame.
    O rare, &c.

His nerues or sinewes like Bulls pissles,
    for riding rods some vse:
Of Spermaceti there's some vessels:
    if this be the worst newes,
That of this monster we shall heare,
All will be well I doe not feare.
    O rare, &c.

Already sixteene tuns of Oyle
    is from this fish extracted,
And yet continually they boyle,
    no season is protracted:

It cannot be imagin'd how much
'Twill yeeld, the vastnesse on't is such.
    O rare, &c.

When he vpon the sands was cast
    aliue, which was awhile:
He yell'd so loud, that many (agast)
    heard him aboue sixe mile:
Tis said the Female fish likewise
Was heard to mourne with horrid cryes:
    O rare, &c.

The Mariners of Chester *say*
    a Herring-hog tis nam'd:
Whatere it be, for certaine they
    that are for knowledge fam'd,
Affirme, the like in ages past
Upon our Coast was neuer cast.
    O rare
    beyond compare,
  in England nere the like.

M.P.

Printed at London for *Thomas Lambert*, at the sign of the Hors-shoo in Smith-field. *There is a Book to satisfie such as desire a larger description hereof.*

THIS BROADSIDE ballad was written in the early 1630s by Martin Parker, in his time the leading practitioner in the art and trade of balladmongering.[1] Street ballads, sung and sold printed on sheets of paper in the streets of London, are known to have existed for at least four centuries,

102

roughly from the invention of printing to the invention of the phonograph. It is not known exactly when the first ballads were
printed, but Hyder Rollins argues that "the street ballad was ma-
tured as early as 1500," and he cites the Oxford bookseller John
Dorne who in 1520 had a stock of more than a hundred and ninety
ballads.[2] Parker's career belongs to the time of the greatest vigor
and importance of street ballads, and his surviving work, more
extensive than that of any competitor, is a fair sampling of the
spectrum of such ballads: war news; jests on husbands, wives,
and whores; advice to lovers; sober salute to honest labor; satire
of all trades; satire of marital patterns; sensational and senten-
tious accounts of infanticide, black magic, and various other
alarms.[3]

The broadside ballad embodies a set of contradictions, which
give it an obvious ungainliness fairly represented by Parker's
beached whale. The verses of a broadside, printed on paper, are a
commodity in trade. The author writes to sell, and the buyer buys
both to read and to sing, to fit them to a tune specified by the
author but already in the buyer's possession. The ballads were
really sung, as well as being put up on walls. (See the customers
of Autolycus in *The Winter's Tale*.) When the new owner sings
them they will exist in a different medium and for different purposes from their medium and purpose when they are the author's
wares in the hawker's basket. Like any article of commerce, that
is to say, they must be adapted to two roles, serve two purposes,
which meet at the moment of sale and purchase. They must be
calculated to sell, and they must at least seem contrived to serve
the purchaser.

Caveat emptor. The selling is a crossing of crossed purposes.
Any buyer may be disappointed with his trinket, discovering how
shallowly his desired colors have been painted over the substance
of the seller's interests. The magnitude of the conflict is attested
by the exertions of advertising, whose whole business is to deny
it. In the present case, the product is verbal and acts as its own
advertisement while it is the seller's, but it is to be the song of the
buyer when it is his. The question here is, whose words are they?

The question remains relevant as long as there is a song business, and it is especially well displayed in the case of the street ballad. In antiquity and in the Middle Ages professional singers had sold their performances.[4] Here, for the first time, an author sells his song, and the separation of writing from singing by commerce produces instructive violations of the tact we generally presume in a songwriter.

A conflict is betrayed by any intrusion of an author into his song, by which he admits a potentially adversarial distance from his audience. Such traces remain as awkward implications that any singer of the verses is a dummy on the knee of the writer. Parker was sometimes aware of the conflict. In another ballad, "A Banquet for Sovereign Husbands," he sought to resolve it by using his salesman as a persona:

If here be any scolding wives
I wish them if they love their lives
In any case not buy this song,
Which doth to gentle wives belong.
Thus from the Author told I am,
who made this ditty of the Ram.[5]

He performed a similar voice-casting in some satirical ballads, as in "A He-Devil" where the speaker is the victimized wife: "I like a servile bond-slave, / doe wipe his boots and shooes . . ."[6]

But in "A Description of a Strange Fish" the conflict is simple and overt. "But here's a stranger . . . Invites my pen"; "let the Writer beare no blame." Parker, who took the role of poet and pamphleteer in other literary projects, here produces an avowed writing. Each admission is a flaw when the consumer attempts to set the verses to the tune of *Bragandary*. Besides these trespasses, some of the grammatical and logical quirks of the text may reflect the same uneasiness of ballad author seeking the proper relationship to his public. The opening lines, "Of many marvels in my time / I've heretofore," seem to be missing some two-syllable verb that would have constituted another self-display of authorship but that has been somehow repressed. (The most likely mechanism would be haplography of "I've *heard of here-tofore*" by either author or typesetter.) Stanza nine appeals, "Then let's with charity confess / God's works are more then man can guess"; *charity* is not the right word for reverential awe, but it is the right word for what one needs in order to get into that mood, past suspicious incredulity of our fellow man, the author, who is peddling these wonders. It comes as a protestation, out of the same defensiveness as the disclaimer ("let the Writer beare no blame") in stanza eleven; it makes no sense once the song is the owner's own song. In stanza four, the jostling of our Potent Lord with Neptune for jurisdiction over the beast is brought about by the irrepressible urge to work in a classical allusion on the part of the writer whose literary self defiantly interrupts the business of songwriting.

Yet for the most part Parker does construct a working song, a piece of goods that can in fact please the customer. The ballad takes the shape required by the function it has for the buyer; or, to admit the tautology, we can read what it offers the buyer in the way it is built.

Rollins writes that the ballads "were, in the main, the equivalent of modern newspapers . . ."; their final decline has been tied to the abolition in 1855 of the stamp duty and the consequent rise of the cheap newspaper.[7] The comparison is most helpful if we add, giving serious journalism the benefit of a doubt, that the equivalence is specifically with sensational journalism, and if we remember that the business of sensational journalism is sensations. We generally think that we buy the news in order to open ourselves to an inflow of miscellaneous information. But this is clearly not always so. If a news headline says, "Police Search Swamp for More Bodies," we may snatch up the paper to read for some moments just what that headline promised: that there is no development in the awful case of those murders announced to us yesterday. The reading offers no significant new facts (if there were new facts, why would we need to know them?), but it does provide a chance to indulge in a trailing wave of the excitement of yesterday, when we were first titillated by a gory report. We are willing to pay money to possess the account. We may even buy a second paper to have a competing account of the same failure of anything new to happen, because our object is not information but excitement, and a new configuration of words on the same ostensible subject is as good as a new configuration on a new subject.

It would seem to be a good sign that it is an amusement rather than a lesson that invites us when a headline approaches in some way equivalence to text, so that we must confess to knowing ahead of time what we are reading to find out. In Smollett's *Roderick Random* the table of contents tells the entire story, in notes also printed severally at the heads of the chapters—chapter 67, for example, is only fourteen paragraphs long, and is preceded by an eighty-seven word headnote—so there is no suspense in Smollett's invitation to us to savor several-score instances of Roderick getting even with someone. Similarly, some of the broadsides give twice whatever they have to give in the way of information. In the Bagford collection one ballad offers itself as

> THE MARINERS MISFORTUNE; OR, THE UNFORTUNATE VOYAGE OF TWO CONSTANT LOVERS. Being an Account of a faithful Seaman, who going to take his Farewel of his Sweetheart, she resolved come Life, or come Death, to Sail with him; and putting her self into Mans Apparel, went the Voyage with him, but by distress of weather, coming home were cast away, the constant Seaman having no other help, betook himself to swimming, and having got his Sweetheart upon his back, swam till he was almost tyred, but was at last taken up by an Algerine, who carryed them to *Algiers*, where being brought before the Governour, she confessed her selfe to be a Female, which so astonished the Governour, that he in requital of her constancy, set them both free, who are happily Arrived in *England* again.[8]

The street ballads, often with woodcuts that anticipate the photography of modern sensational journalism, typically advertise themselves graphically and typographically so well that no surprise can come out of the text.

Furthermore they were sung in the street by the vendor, so that their whole report was available to the buyer before he bought. Once one has heard the song itself, it is idle to pretend that one buys the ballad to learn about the strange fish. Buying shows the buyer's desire not merely to learn the facts but to take possession of them. Owning the ballad confers certain proprietary rights and opportunities. The new owner can, for example, take it back to the tavern with him and amaze a circle of listeners.

But the proprietary relationship of owner to ballad is more basic than simply the chance it offers to pass the excitement on in turn to someone else. The satisfaction made available by this ownership is a bit like that of owning some stock in the monster, the right to suspend disbelief and riot in credulity. Why would your own ballad lie to you? Mopsa says, "I love a ballad in print, a-life, for then we are sure they are true." What there is to buy in the ballad is attested by the curiously garbled headnote: "A description of a strange . . . fish, cast upon the sands. . . . The certainty whereof is here related concerning the said most monstrous fish." The words say less than they may seem to. "The certainty that this fish exists" or "the certainty that this fish was cast up at such a place" is related about this fish. About this fish is related its certainty. This "Description" will now assert for certain that it is certain. This fish story will now claim to be true.

This carelessly padded phrasing is not inaccurate, because as song what the ballad offers is not so much things related about the fish as certainty about it, a mental state upon encounter with the idea of fish-monster, a mind-set toward the purported facts. The ballad stanza by stanza does bring before us one fact after another, often with associated numbers to support their evidentiary gravity. But as we come to one stanza after another there can be little sense of filling in the picture of the whole, little perspective in which the facts group together to form an understanding; we get only the assurance that one more part of it is also mighty big. The tongue is worth a stanza, but the function is filled when the stanza says only, "the same goes for the tongue":

The tongue on't is so mighty large
  I will it not expresse,
Lest I your credit ouer-charge,
  but you may easily guesse,
That sith his shape so far excels,
The tongue doth answer all parts else.

The stanza is one more way to work up to the chorus, "O rare / Beyond compare, / In England nere the like." The function of each stanza as the ballad gropes its way around the beast is best announced in the pissle stanza: "This monster he who well regards, / from th' first unto the last, / By every part may motives find, / To wonder at this wondrous kind."

The ballad as sensational journalism offers fifteen occasions to indulge in wonder. Owning it is less like owning a fact-sheet than it is like owning a book of pin-up photographs or dirty stories, to which one returns at will for the excitation of a special state of feeling. But as it is song it does not work exactly like titillation in any other medium. It works by giving the singer who takes possession of it, in hand or memory, the chance not only to hear of the whale but to testify about it; and the satisfaction of testifying is not merely that of passing along the wonder, but of experiencing the wonder firsthand, of declaring the glory of whales.

The whale has been a standard wonder, and not only in the seventeenth century. Melville opens *Moby-Dick* with a playful catalogue of "Extracts (Supplied by Sub-Sub-Librarian)" to show the enduring fascination of the beast, to which we might add for present reference the famous print by Goltzius in 1598 of a *Whale Washed Ashore in Holland*, such pamphlets as the one announced at the foot of this ballad, and the learned study in the *Philosophical Transactions* of the Royal Society (1693) "Of the Whale's Pizzle, and its Use in Physick" (cited by the *OED*, s.v. "pizzle"). This last instance has distinct relevance to the preoccupation of the broadside, declared by the huge sexual member displayed in the woodcut and by repeated references in the stanzas. The shape of the whale illustrated is itself phallic, and some of the wonders catalogued by the ballad seem to have a congruence to that shape—the tongue, the teeth, the jawbone given as a jutting length—in addition to the pissle, the cods, the nerves or sinews like bull's pissles, and the vessels of spermaceti. (The woodcut gives a similar erected tongue to the monster in the water, but she is the bereaved, or deprived, female "heard to mourne with horrid cryes.") That phallic symbolism attaches easily to whales is manifested by the long confusion over the nature of spermaceti oil and suggests one quality to the fascination in the spectacle of an exposed whale carcass. In the ballad it contributes an infusion of phallic boasting or admiring to the wonder indulged in by a singer. There is in any case a certain boasting quality in all marveling, especially marveling to others in company. We have a proprietary interest in the wonder we can point out or attest, and we claim some credit for it. But again, the satisfaction of communicating wonder is secondary when the boast is a song. The primary satisfaction is wonder itself.

To the modern mind it may not seem strange that the city and country populace of earlier centuries had songs about what interested them, or that they had journalism about it, so much as that they sang their journalism. Yet the variety of song-journalism represented by the "Description of a Strange Fish" ran long and deep in the history of English popular culture. What appears to us to be a curious hybrid form met a strong and lasting demand. Considering the meaning of that demand takes us back to the physical psychology of how words relate to tunes.

From the mid-1500s to the late 1600s, when the fashion developed of printing musical notation on the sheet along with the ballad verses, the broadside ballad typically carried a note either that the ballad should be sung "To the tune of X," naming or quoting a song already popular, or that it went "To a pleasant new tune." These latter new tunes are mysteries now but were not so for their buyers, who heard the tunes from the street seller of the broadsides.[9] All the tunes were tunes familiar to the buyer before he bought. Contrariwise, all that was said in a ballad was protested to be new, because the ballads were articles in commerce, and the necessary pretense of sale is that one gives up money to gain goods one does not already possess. Thus for the sixteenth and seventeenth centuries, the broadside ballads were new words to old music, or, more exactly, they were the latest new words to go with known music already in the mind of the prospective buyer.

No one would expect that such cheap goods as these penny ballads should show much artistry in the sense of disciplined, discriminating craft. Sophisticated writers did dabble in ballad-making, but the typical ballad will not be expected to have been much concerned with fine proprieties of what is said and how it is said or of how the words are accommodated to the named music. The ballads are fitted to their music with loose comfort: Rollins mentions some that announce themselves to be suited to two or more tunes. The singer was entrusted with most of the close accommodating of the verses to the tune. Claude Simpson says, when he has printed a slur in the musical notation of a broadside tune because it was shown in its source to fit two or more notes to a syllable, that it may "fit an initial stanza but not succeeding ones, and rarely is the pattern completely suitable for singing other songs."[10]

Little stress can be laid on how a broadside tune gives expressiveness to its verses in any sense where they need to be peculiarly appropriate to each other. The ballad-makers did sometimes show some consistency in matching tune character to mood of verse. Simpson notes that the "stately strains of 'Fortune my foe' are . . . frequently . . . coupled with solemn or lugubrious accounts of murders, natural disaster, warnings to the impious, deathbed confessions, and the like."[11] On the other hand, very disparate ballads, a whole spectrum of kinds of ballads, might be set to one tune. The even more popular tune "Packington's Pound" is specified for over a hundred known ballads, and "there is almost no limit to the variety of subjects treated in 'Packington's

Pound' ballads."[12] They range, to take casual examples, from "The Praise of the Dairy-Maid" to "The History of the Prophet Jonas."

The casualness in the matter of the setting of words to music in broadside ballads invites us to pose the question of what service the tune was called on to render for the ballad-maker or his audience. The reason for people wanting to sing the tunes, even to sing them so many times, is a bigger question that I do not mean to raise here, except to acknowledge the importance and worth of the experience of singing in itself. It is not surprising that the ballad public enjoyed its music. Allowing that the songs were enjoyed partly because people simply liked the tunes, we can still ask just what role the old tune plays in the new ballad. What does it mean for the ballad-maker to choose a familiar tune to fit his verses to and for the customer to give money for some new words to the tune he already knows? .

When a song takes over the music from some previous song also known to those who sing or hear the new song, what can we say most generally and essentially remains of the old experience in the new? The constant minimum, I think, is simply the knowing how it goes. The familiar tune contributes familiarity. More complicated interactions of what belongs to one song and what belongs to the other are possible, but they imply reflective consciousness apart from the proper experience of the familiar melody, often occuring before and after the singing itself. Reflections on the ironic change of parody or of moralization, for example, are certainly possible even during singing but are sophistications superadded to the essential and often the only effect of an old tune's familiarity—that the audience has an assured sense of how it goes. This tiny minimum, however, has real significance.

Consider again the large history of the broadside ballad. Such ballads constituted, as Rollins says, the chief publications of the London press, at least in the reigns of Mary and Elizabeth. They were known to everyone and sold to an audience stretching far beyond the small circle of those who bought books. The buying public for ballads was not otherwise a reading public: before the rise of the printing trade it had read nothing. Yet that trade found in ballads a way to sell it a steady supply of printed words. They became customers for reading matter when words were printed for a tune, a familiar tune; the music of the ballad mediated the reading of print for most of the total public the printers reached. Buying the products of the printing press means taking possession of someone else's words fixed onto paper, which one proposes to read, that is, to make into the words of one's own vocal or subvocal speech. Fully literate readers do this reverse ventriloquism with ease and confidence. We may imagine, however, that for the large and enduring public of the broadside ballads the naming of a tune that the words promised to fit was a significant help, a significant inducement to buy printed words. Knowing the tune is an assurance: it is knowing ahead of time, and in the reading process itself, how the words go, how they will come out in the cadence of one's own voice. It is also, incidentally, a great boost to memorization, so that the words can be returned to, for whatever they have to offer, without the labor of rereading.

The continual return of each day's ballads to the previous day's tunes is intimately connected with the odd fact that so much of the production of the Renaissance printing press invoked music. The significance of these two facts taken together can be more fully stated in the terms of brain function introduced in the preceding chapter. A tune is perceived, held in memory, and called up for the voice by the nondominant right cerebral hemisphere. In nonliterate culture, verbal structures such as ballads (if not also the ordinary uses of words in daily affairs) are highly patterned by formulas and by further, elaborate grouping and bracketing patterns that are only recently being fully recognized by students of oral literature. These structures, like tunes, are the sign of greater involvement of the right hemisphere in the making and experiencing of oral literature than is found in the mental processes of literacy with its discipline to linear writing and reading. The change in mentality from nonliterate to literate is profound; it involves an importantly different coordination of two basic kinds of thinking that go on in the human mind.

The broadside ballad is a great meeting ground of orality and literacy. Defined as it is by bought printed words to be processed by the left hemisphere and familiar tune to be recalled out of the right, it represents a long intermediate stage of mental accommodation on the road to a literate society.

6

Theater Song: "Oh, Ponder Well"

Oh, ponder well! Be not severe;
  So save a wretched wife!
For on the rope that hangs my dear
  Depends poor Polly's life.

O H, PONDER WELL" is the twelfth of sixty-nine songs in John Gay's *The Beggar's Opera*. James Boswell was told that James Quin, an actor who had declined the lead in the play, said

> that during the first night of its appearance it was long in a very dubious state; that there was a disposition to damn it, and that it was saved by the song,
>
>   "Oh ponder well! be not severe!"
>
> the audience being much affected by the innocent looks of Polly, when she came to those two lines, which exhibit at once a painful and ridiculous image,
>
>   "For on the rope that hangs my Dear,
>   Depends poor Polly's life."[1]

Boswell's criticism here is as valuable as his gossip. The "painful and ridiculous" quality he detects in the image reflects the compounded nature of the whole play, at once sentimental and satirical; it is the distinctive mixture that brought the work its huge popular success.

Gay had struck the same note in other writings, some of them songs. His early piece called "Sweet William's Farewell to Black-ey'd Susan: A Ballad" does a skillful job of promoting the same effect through gently mocking pastoral: William the sailor and his

sweetheart take leave of each other with courtly words and gestures, rendered in courtly figures of speech:

> *If to far* India's *coast we sail,*
>   *Thy eyes are seen in di'monds bright,*
> *Thy breath is* Africk's *spicy gale,*
>   *Thy skin is ivory, so white.*
> *Thus ev'ry beauteous object that I view,*
> *Wakes in my soul some charm of lovely* Sue.

With this treatment of lower-class lovers Gay had offered his
readers both endearing sentiment and amusement. He and his
readers indulge in benign condescension to the appealing innocence of the lovers and obtain a double satisfaction: we are superior to these clownish figures, and we are also superior to cynicism about them, which would be defensive, and can savor their
sweet sentiments. The trick is a manipulation of point of view,
elaborate for a song, where some of the narrative is third-person,
assuring distance, but the expressions of love on both parts are
spoken as the voices of one and then the other lover.

   The Beggar's Opera is a different blend of the same elements.
It is said to have been pastoral in conception, implying the satis-
factions proper to that sophisticated form. William Empson, the
most acute and difficult critic of pastoral, says of the play, "Indeed the audience did not want to despise heroic and pastoral but
to enjoy them without feeling cheated."[2] It is central to Gay's work
that he somehow negotiates for us the right to mock and to indulge
at the same time. *The Beggar's Opera* is clearly satirical and has
been so understood from its first night. Indeed it is universally
satirical. Pope remarked that it was "a piece of Satire which hit
all tastes and degrees of men, from those of the highest Quality to
the very Rabble"[3]—it attacks the ministry, the court, merchants,
outlaws, whores, virgins, and opera stars. Yet it was universally
applauded, proving Swift's dictum that satire is a sort of glass
wherein beholders do generally discover everybody's face but

their own. The satire implies distance between us and the characters, distance down. Yet the play is also deeply sentimental, able,
as Boswell said, to cause its audience to be temporarily much affected. Gay's principal device for making this happen—the rush
of sentiment despite the satire—is his use of songs.

A song, set in a play, but set out of the play too by its music,
facilitates our indulgence in feelings that may be undercut before
and after the music plays. It is a versatile device for the stage
writer, because the song parenthesis can keep sentiment either in
or out. "Oh, Ponder Well" is sentimental in a cynical context.
Contrarily, a satirical song may be sung by some rowdy in an otherwise tender or serious dramatic context, allowing a momentary
indulgence in a cynical mood, from which we return easily to se-
riousness. (The effect is worked without music in the rousing bar-
racks-song of the soldiers in Auden's spoken oratorio *For the Time
Being*, just before they massacre the innocents.) *The Beggar's Opera* includes songs of both sentiment and cynicism, so that in a
recital of the songs alone Gay's characteristic blend of feelings
could be appreciated.

But Boswell rightly analyzes this one song as capturing both
feelings, offering pleasing pain denatured by a touch of the ridiculous. Polly at her most appealing is not untouched by irony. The
range of attitudes offered by Gay's songs is not so wide as to leave
his performance a recital of random moods. The range is wide:
Peachum sings cynicism, Polly sings self-pity, Macheath sings
bravado, Polly sings indignation. The audience takes each of
these songs for its own, while each lasts, in an identification not
limited to identification with the various characters. No one sees
himself as Peachum, but anyone can lend himself to Peachum's
song:

The priest calls the lawyer a cheat;
  The lawyer be-knaves the divine;
And the statesman, because he's so great
  Thinks his trade as honest as mine.

What we take to heart is the jolly and self-excusingly cynical mood Peachum displays and the familiar sort of self-protective accusations he throws around. Partly because the sometimes outrageous sentiments of the people in the drama are matched to catchy tunes, they catch us into them. When Polly sings "Oh, Ponder Well" she allows her audience to savor a special sentimentality, native to the play and to the age that produced it, a sentimentality harmonious with the other moods of the play: each of those other moods also is somehow an indulgence with the reservation of some small self-irony. Polly's sentiment here, defined not by who Polly is elsewhere in the play (shrewish, witty, comic) but by the words themselves of this song, is sentiment to which irony contributes flavor.

Before the words are considered in detail, it should be asked how far their effect is directed or even constituted by the music to which they are set. Gay's choice of his music is probably the most significant side of his play. Percy Scholes, who mistakenly follows Charles Burney in attributing the selection of music to Gay's arranger Pepusch, credits it with significant influence not only in the theater but on musical history. He claims, under the heading of "Influence of the Ballad Opera," that beyond its beginning a fad for ballad opera that ended a fad for Italian opera, "a feature of song production . . . during the eighteenth century is the perpetuation, in what we may call the professional repertory, of many of the qualities of the folksong—simple verse-repeating tunes being greatly in vogue as a result of the popularity of [this] form of opera."[4]

Gay wrote all of his songs to popular song tunes of the day. He was not the first musical playwright to do so: D'Urfey wrote many stage songs to ballad airs, and Shakespeare may have done the same. Ballad tunes are specified as the music for songs in the mid-sixteenth-century *Commodye of pacient and meeke Grissill.*[5] But the full ballad opera begins with Gay, and considerable attention has been paid to the way he moved from an old song to a new one. Bertrand Bronson examines the reminiscences of several

original songs in lyrics Gay wrote, and observes, "A large major-
ity of the tunes he chose were associated with amorous words, and
not infrequently Gay kept phrases, refrain lines or half lines, or
followed the earlier verbal patterns, for his new lyrics. There is
no doubt that he thus won the amused attention of all whose tastes
had made them familiar with the originals."[6] Yvonne Noble takes
these musical allusions to be influential in right understanding of
the whole play. "The continual presence of such tunes in *The
Beggar's Opera* argues strongly to the audience, with the compelling logic of association, in favor of Macheath's amorous generosity over the unkindly restraint implied in Polly's self-conscious
innocence."[7]

It must be questioned how far such allusion generally operates
in the experience of songs. Bronson cites a D'Urfey song against
marriage given a subtle transformation and says, "Remembrance
of these words gives additional piquancy to Mrs. Peachum's praise
of marriage. Only *after* a woman is married, she declares, does
she win freedom."[8] Assuming D'Urfey's song was well known to
much of the audience, which is likely, it seems to me very unlikely that this subtle change was much appreciated. Even well-
known words, grown as it seems organically into their musical
phrasing, so that they will mutter insistently at the back of one's
vacant mind, are remarkably elusive of attention if we are giving
any attention to other words presented to the same music. The
borrowing or ironical conversion of lines from older songs shows
us the path taken by Gay's creativity as he fashioned a new song
for his play. But comparative examination of two texts as one is
heard and the other is to be summoned by memory, however of-
ficious and automatic that memory may be in the idle mind, is not
easy. Consider the case of the moralized ballad. Rollins, in his
study of broadside ballads, says that among those ballads

> moralizations abounded, parodies that followed the original
> ballad closely in diction and exactly in metre and stanza-
> form, but gave to the subject-matter a pious and religious
> twang. As early as 1525 John Skot had printed "The New Nut-

Brown Maid upon the Passion of Christ." . . . Every ballad-monger tried his hand at it.[9]

If interference of old words with new were ever to occur, we might expect it to subvert any such pious labor with good old ribaldry; but if such subversion did happen, it was not such as to discourage a universal optimism among these writers for the conversion of the devil's good tunes. Similarly we owe our Christmas carols to the fully successful effort to drive out an old coinage of licentious holiday songs; although no records show whether tunes were impressed and converted, nothing is more likely. (A late example is William Dix's Victorian hymn "What Child Is This?", in which the new words written to the plaintive chorus of the old love song are made stirringly affirmative—"This, this is Christ the King." The hymn seems to carry very little reminiscence of "Greensleeves," although perhaps here the two sets of feelings are simply irrelevant to each other.)

Certainly a tune may bring with it a distinctive mood, and that mood can be further defined by words and lines retained from the predecessor song, especially an opening line. But the way music builds the effect of any given text is little affected by its previous marriages to other words. It is only speculative to argue how things worked in the minds of the Londoners who knew Gay's tunes, but Gay's great success with his musical experiment surely came principally because he invited his audience to enjoy, in a satirical context that allowed them to continue to think of themselves as sophisticated, the simple tunes they enjoyed anyway, in relief perhaps from the harder pleasures of the fashionable foreign-language opera.

What is usefully reinforcing to Gay's new songs from the old tunes is their familiarity itself, not the refined aptness of their old roles to their new casting. In the most general terms, music always bears up and seconds what its words say in that it lends them its good form. It is a validation of song words, which say for us something we want them to say, that they come out right, to the pattern of the music as it finds its resolution in whatever makes good form within a particular musical style. When the tune is already known to us, our apprehension of it as carrying the words to a fitting resolution is already prepared.

The tune of Air XII in Gay's text is announced as *Now Ponder Well, Ye Parents Dear*, the opening words of an old ballad generally called "The Children in the Wood," a lamentable tragedy praised by Addison, which in *Percy's Reliques* runs to twenty double stanzas. It begins,

Now ponder well, you parents deare
  These wordes which I shall write;
A doleful story you shall hear
  In time brought forth to light.

The connection of old and new words is less close here than in other airs in the play. The popularity of the sad old song offered Gay a chance to write Polly an appeal to parents, with impetus to be borrowed from the first half-line. Simpson, in his exhaustive study of the tunes of the broadside ballads, notes that this tune was called for eventually in nineteen ballad operas during the boom that followed 1728.[10] Gay showed his contemporaries what a serviceable tune it was; his success with it seems not to have encumbered it with associations to interfere with its further adventures.

The small initial borrowing of words, upon which Gay built the small remainder of the text, gives at once the characteristic posture of the lyric. The posture is a droop. It is given in the feeble expostulation of the sense, in the feeble discharge of the *p* consonant abandoning its bilabial stop of the breath (the sound returns three times in the climactic last line), and in the descent of the tune to the tonic in regular little steps after a listless rising gesture. In the key of F, the notes are GAG*F* / GAG*F* / AB♭DCAG // AB♭DC / B♭CA*F* / CDFAG*F*, as the tune droops to the floor of its tonic note four times and almost five. The second half-line of text deprecates severity in sheer submission. The second whole line refrains from petitioning for anything in particular,

AIR XII. Now ponder well, ye Parents dear.

Polly. *Oh, ponder well! be not severe;*
So save a wretched Wife!
For on the Rope that hangs my Dear
Depends poor Polly's *Life.*

promising that Polly will be saved if those with power (she has none but helplessness) merely restrain their will to harm.

The remainder of the lyric constitutes the image that Boswell found "at once . . . painful and ridiculous." The ridiculousness centers around the near-pun in *depends*, whose Latin root was active in the educated ear of the time, contributing its literal sense of *hangs down*. The literalization presses forward in the absence of any very good nonliteral sense: it is not exactly accurate that her life *depends* in the abstract sense on the rope, more the reverse—if the rope hangs her husband, she seems to intend to say, her life is over as well; so properly her life depends abstractly on there not being a rope that hangs her love. What Boswell must have found ridiculously improper is the stark intrusion of the hanging lump of life, which is also lifeless, or about to be lifeless, thrown into relief in the Latin shadow cast by the verb.

Someone is manipulating the language here with a certain archness. Of course it is Gay, and then Polly sings his words. Coming from Gay they are a bit playful. Coming from Polly they touch her with a self-consciousness that detaches her slightly

Words and music for "Air XII" from John Gay's *The Beggar's Opera* are reproduced by permission of the Beinecke Rare Book and Manuscript Library, from the John Christopher Pepusch collection of plays (1728).

from her predicament, the irony we have alluded to above. The detachment is perhaps easier to see when it is considered that she is singing about herself in the third person. Her mood is not despair or even agitation, but rather the tranquility of self-pity, where the self is conceived objectively as suffering for its virtues but seen from a serene elevation.

Polly's deprecation of a cruel fate is charming, where to charm me is to disarm my aggressive impulses, my suspicion and cynicism, by a gesture of self-offering. Like any bowing of the head, Polly's drooping is a ritual of declaring vulnerability. She invokes the taboo against harming the helpless and so appeals to be taken under my protection. If I am the Duke of Bolton her self-offering is irresistible. "Lavinia Fenton . . . who acted Polly, married the third Duke of Bolton. She had three sons by him before marriage. . . . Dr. Warton . . . adds that the air that saved the Opera 'is said irresistibly to have conquered the lover who afterwards married her.'"[11]

But if one special effect of her singing self-pity was to invite the duke to an identification of point of view such that he also took pity on her virtuous self, more generally the song opens to its audience an exquisite moment of disinterested self-pity, an ecstasy above the self to savor its lovely sadness from not too close. The self here, indeed anyone's self considered as martyred to its pure fidelity, is something of a mirage, a virtual image, so that elevation above it is a good deal like sheer elevation. In a brilliant study of the sentiments of literature in the Age of Sensibility, Northrop Frye finds them to include "pity without an object."[12] The elevation above a fictive self that Polly allows us to share comes close to that description.

Religious Song: "Love Divine, All Loves Excelling"

Love Divine, all Loves excelling,
  Joy of Heaven to Earth come down,
Fix in us thy humble Dwelling,
  All thy faithful Mercies crown;
JESU, Thou art all Compassion,
  Pure unbounded Love Thou art,
Visit us with thy Salvation,
  Enter every trembling Heart.

Breathe, O breathe thy loving Spirit
  Into every troubled Breast,
Let us all in Thee inherit,
  Let us find that Second Rest:
Take away our Power of sinning,
  Alpha and Omega be,
End of Faith as its Beginning,
  Set our Hearts at Liberty.

Come, Almighty to deliver,
  Let us all thy Life receive,
Suddenly return, and never,
  Never more thy Temples leave.
Thee we would be always blessing,
  Serve Thee as thy Hosts above.
Pray, and praise Thee without ceasing,
  Glory in thy perfect Love.

Finish then thy New Creation,
  Pure and sinless let us be,
Let us see thy great Salvation,
  Perfectly restor'd in Thee;
Chang'd from Glory into Glory,
  Till in Heaven we take our Place,
Till we cast our Crowns before Thee,
  Lost in Wonder, Love, and Praise.

N THE FOURTH CENTURY Athanasius, Bishop of Alexandria, wrote a pastoral letter analyzing the peculiar benefits offered by the Book of Psalms in comparison with other scripture. "The Lord," he wrote, "wishing the melody of the words to be a symbol of the spiritual harmony in a soul, has ordered . . . the Psalms recited with song." Consequently there is "this astonishing thing" in the Psalms: he who takes up this book "recognizes . . . his own words. And the one who hears is deeply moved, as though he himself were speaking, and is affected by the words of the songs, as if they were his own songs." In the rest of the Bible, we consider ourselves to be other than those about whom the passage speaks; but "he who recites the Psalms is uttering [them] as his own words, and each sings them as if they were written concerning himself." The worshiper who appropriates the words of the psalter in this way appropriates divinely inspired words, and he rises above his ordinary self: the soul, "gaining its composure by the singing of the phrases . . . becomes forgetful of the passions and, while rejoicing, sees in accordance with the mind of Christ."[1] Athanasius argued that only scriptural words could exalt in this way, but by his argument it can be seen that even in his own time some of the numerous Christians of whom he disapproved were setting other words to music for church song.

Charles Wesley published this modern hymn in 1747. He and his brother John, the founders of Methodism, brought about a great flowering of English hymns in the eighteenth century, Charles as writer and John mainly as editor. Many other Englishmen, including their father and an older brother, had written hymns. The dissenter Isaac Watts had produced a significant body of hymn verse in the first half of the century, including hymns for children. John Wesley, however, collected the first hymnal for use in the Church of England in 1737, and in the subsequent fifty years Charles, who remained a minister of that church, created the immensely popular core of a permanent hymnody for the new Methodism, and for English-speaking Protestants generally.[2] At his death he had published 4,480 hymns in over fifty collections, and he had written half as many again. One student of his work figures that Wesley wrote a quantity of extant verse the equivalent of ten lines every day for fifty years. From this huge mass the tiny fraction still sung is yet some hundreds of hymns. From the major Protestant denominational hymn books approved for congregational use in the twentieth century, an index lists 252 songs by Wesley. "Love Divine" appears in fifty-eight such books, that is, in practically all except the hymnals of the Unitarians, Mormons, Christian Scientists, and Mennonites.[3]

The spreading of these hymns through the world and their duration through two centuries give only two dimensions of Charles Wesley's contribution to the religious life of a very large number of people. The third dimension is depth, the active involvement of the individual worshiper that follows from the nature of congregational song as song. The present hymn, like many hymns but unlike most other songs, is cast in the first person plural. The whole proper audience are presumed to be the singers. It is not necessary to judge the art or doctrine of a hymn to allow that, since the hymn furnishes the words of active participatory worship for each member of the church, it will be an integral part of such worship, as compared, say, to the more chancy intervention of sermon. Choral anthems and solo singing have also had a prominent place in many kinds of worship, but hymns such as this one necessarily inform religious experience to a greater extent. Any song sung before the congregation, appropriated like other songs to its audience, does offer its words up on their behalf ("And the one who hears is deeply moved, . . . as if they were his own songs"); but the song actually sung by the whole church imposes itself upon the worshipers in a more peremptory way. When it is sung outside the church—for example, by families, as was the custom among early Methodists—it makes a congregation of the singers present, and orders a part of their private worship. (Wesley published a collection for home use, *Hymns for Families*, in 1767.)

The apostle Paul wrote the Ephesians commending "speaking to yourselves in psalms and hymns and spiritual songs" (5:19). Whether a hymn addresses God in prayer, as this one does, or whether it addresses single or collective self, or some indefinite third party in testimony, hymn verse gives the congregation words to speak to itself. Hymns are, among other things, didactic. The Wesleys certainly saw their hymns this way. John called his brother's work "a body of . . . practical divinity" in his preface to the major collection in 1780, and a theologian has devoted a book to the evangelical doctrines of Charles Wesley's hymns. Concern that this particular hymn might not be teaching strictly proper doctrine in one phrase led John to edit out the second stanza after 1780; emendations have been made to that stanza by subsequent editors. But while Charles Wesley taught carefully some doctrines rather than others, like other reformers of Christianity from Martin Luther to William Blake he saw what he was doing as rendering the basic Christian truth from the basic Christian source: that is, he was teaching the Bible.

> His verse is an enormous sponge filled to saturation with Bible words, Bible similes, Bible metaphors, Bible stories, Bible themes. In the thirty-two lines of "With glorious clouds incompast round" Dr. W. F. Moulton found references to no fewer than fifty verses of scripture. Indeed, in the memorable words of Dr. J. E. Rattenbury, "A skilful man, if the Bible were lost, might extract much of it from Wesley's hymns. They contain the Bible in solution."[4]

The Bible is the repertoire of words, phrases, and thoughts from which Wesley as songwriter builds his verse, as opposed, for example, to eighteenth-century poetic diction, which he rarely uses, though it appears in John Wesley's hymns and translations.[5] As single words the language is obviously Bible and church lan-

guage, the nouns and verbs and adjectives of King James scripture, and hence of sermon, prayer, and religious talk and writing
generally: in the first stanza, *joy, mercies, compassion, visit, salvation,* and less obviously *fix, dwelling, trembling.* Likewise from
the English Bible, of course, are the archaic formal pronouns and
verbs of address, still current in much Protestant prayer.

The phrase "Love Divine, all Loves excelling" came to Wesley on the analogy of the "Song of Venus" written by Dryden for
his play *King Arthur,* beginning "Fairest Isle, All Isles Excelling." The melody that Henry Purcell had written for Dryden's
song was christened "Westminster" and recommended for this
hymn when John Wesley published a collection called *Sacred
Melody* in 1761. We can perhaps see here even more clearly than
in Gay's ballad borrowings that no allusion functions in the in-
debtedness to Dryden, any more than in the borrowings Charles
Wesley is believed to have made of the tunes of pub songs.[6] It is
the redundancies with scripture and sermon that work insistently
in the hymn to teach the Christian singer.

Following are some of the echoes of phrases in the English
Bible:

*Joy of Heaven to earth come down: "he which cometh down from
    heaven"* [John 6:33]

Pure unbounded Love Thou art: "God is love" [1 John 4:8
    and also 4:16]

Visit us with thy Salvation: "O visit me with thy salvation" [Ps.
    106:4]

*Breathe, O breathe Thy loving Spirit: "he breathed on them, and
    saith unto them, Receive ye the Holy Ghost"* [John 20:22]

*Alpha and Omega be / End of faith as its beginning: "I am
    Alpha and Omega, the beginning and the end"* [Rev. 22:13]

*Set our Hearts at Liberty: "he hath anointed me . . . to set at
    liberty them that are bruised"* [Luke 4:18]

Suddenly return, and never, / Never more thy Temples leave: "the Lord . . . shall suddenly come to his temple" (Mal. 3:1), combined with New Testament references to the body as temple, such as "your body is the temple of the Holy Ghost" [1 Cor. 6:20]

Thee we would be always blessing: "Giving thanks always for all things unto God" [Eph. 5:20]

Pray, and praise Thee without ceasing: "thank we God without ceasing" [1 Thess. 2:13]

Glory in thy perfect Love: "perfect love casteth out fear" [1 John 4:18]

Pure and sinless [spotless *after 1780*] *let us be:* "a glorious church, not having spot . . . without blemish" [Eph. 5:27]

Let us see thy great Salvation: "mine eyes have seen thy salvation" [Luke 2:30]; "this great salvation in Israel" [1 Sam. 14:45]

Chang'd from Glory into Glory: "we . . . are changed into the same image from glory to glory" [2 Cor. 3:18]

Till we cast our Crowns before Thee: "cast their crowns before the throne" [Rev. 4:10]

Singing the hymn made of such phrases gives and reinforces the lessons of the church, taught to the congregation by itself. They must be short lessons. The line measured to a musical phrase, each of the thirty-two lines of the hymn, carries a message of the moment. The articulation of lines into any longer message is less certain to come home to the singer, as Charles Wesley well knew. His verse is remarkable for the self-containment of single lines. One critic notices that "in general every line contains a complete idea, is in fact a clause or a sentence"; another says that in Wesley "most lines contain one thought and not more than one."[7] In "Love Divine" nearly every line stands by itself.

Only one line lacks punctuation at its end, an odd-numbered line that, in the rhythm of the versification, moves without pause into the even-numbered following line—but again fifteen out of sixteen of these odd-numbered lines, which are not stopped by the rhythm, are marked with grammatical pauses. The even-numbered lines, where the rhythm does pause, are sharply broken off from succeeding lines. Modern editors of the *Methodist Hymnal*, for example, give fourteen out of the sixteen of them at least a semicolon (or colon or period or exclamation mark. Wesley himself was rather fond of exclamation marks). The two mere commas retained in this modern edition, ending stanza three, line 6 and stanza four, line 6, reflect the emotional climaxes prepared in the endings of those two last stanzas: the final couplet of each is an appositive, a heightened repetition of the two lines just before it.

Despite the author's resourcefulness in building his verses to work one by one, some ambiguities may arise when the hymn is sung. One writer suggests that the second line contains "a needless and unintentional ambiguity"—

Love Divine, all Loves excelling,
  Joy of Heaven to Earth come down,

—since "come" may be a petition or a participle ("please come down" or "which has come down").[8] At the end of stanza three, the "Glory" in "Glory in thy perfect Love" may not insist to the singer that it is short for "We would glory"; it might be taken for a noun. In the last stanza,

Let us see thy great Salvation,
  Perfectly restor'd in Thee;

may not make clear who or what is restored—in this case, the better the preceding line is remembered, the more confusion is possible through the suggestion that the salvation is restored, a notion that makes no obvious theological sense. And at the climax of the whole,

Till we cast our Crowns before Thee,
  Lost . . .

it may not be remembered just what must or will happen "till" the
vision from Revelation is realized.

None of these confusions is serious. If they can be made out
as possible by the critical reader, the point of recognizing them is
to see that they do not really matter anyway. Jesus is believed by
the congregation to have come down, and he is also petitioned
here to come down now, into every heart. There is no way to take
"glory" in "perfect love" improperly, even as a noun. Perfect res-
toration of no matter what is no vaguer, or more distracting to the
worshiper, than the "new creation" in "Finish then thy New Creation," just above. It will be argued later that sequence and circumstance are irrelevant to the condition of being "lost" in ecstasy, and not much information is given anyway in the changing
"from Glory into Glory" that is the preparation for that final ecstasy, even if the singer could remember that line from the middle
of the stanza. In other words the nouns, verbs, and participles of
the gospel work reasonably well in these verses to cue the singer's
worship even when the syntax in which they are imbedded is in
any way obscure. The beads are more important than the string.
Wesley has few such faults; other hymnwriters have many more.
Much less well made hymns than this one accomplish their work
acceptably well because the words, phrases, images, and themes
worked into their verses have a scriptural citizenship prior to
their confederation into any particular hymn.

If these considerations imply a relative freedom to be careless
on the part of the hymnwriter, it is to be insisted again that Wesley
is not careless. "Love Divine" is very deliberately built. Despite
the strong emphasis that singing gives to the local features of
verse, a limitation to which this hymn is admirably adapted,
Wesley's art includes craftsmanship on the larger scale as well.
We have said that syntax over more lines than one is easy to forget
and that extended argument evaporates in singing, so that the

hymn in its didactic role must do its work a little at a time. Larger-scale constructive features of the hymn can be understood if we ask what the hymn seeks to do besides teach.

Frank Baker says of Wesley's hymns that no matter with what or where they begin, they end in heaven. "Love Divine" gets there from an opening invocation of divine love to come down. It is organized, then, by two movements, the descent of the divine and the elevation of the faithful, "Till in Heaven we take our Place." The two movements or events are carefully connected, and in fact the hymn works to make it felt that the two are the same. The path is this: "Love come down; fix in us thy dwelling; visit us with salvation. Breathe thy spirit, let us find rest, set our hearts at liberty. Deliver, return, and never leave. We would serve, pray, praise, glory in divine love. Finish thy new creation, perfectly restored, changed, till in heaven we [are] lost in wonder, love, and praise." This sequence as the content of the hymn is not so much an argument as a plot. It is postulated that God defined as love enter each heart, that God as spirit inspire and give peace and liberty, that God as deliverer give grace and bring about perfection; and correlatively, beginning one stanza later, that we inherit and are liberated, passively; that we want to serve, pray, praise, and glory (in ascending sequence), actively; and that when these things arrive at fullness we will be transfigured beyond action to beatitude. Divine action, salvation, is invoked from first to last. As it is imagined to happen, the prayer for grace is increasingly mixed with increasingly vivid realization of what that salvation is: in the first stanza not at all; in the second negatively (rest, not sinning, being freed); in the third, as what we "would"—not might want or will want, but what we do want, beginning with practical service and ending, in anticipation of the next stanza, with glorying; and in the fourth, with a leap to completion that is carefully not made discontinuous as a leap up to heaven but given as intensification of what goes before. We are in heaven, and being there is being lost in wonder, love, and praise.

Like other songs, especially those subject to repetition that may be largely occasional or dutiful, "Love Divine" has had to bear up under abbreviation. A single stanza might be sung, or the first and last. We have noticed that John Wesley cut out the second stanza in 1780. At that time the hymn was already well circulated, so that both three- and four-stanza versions have been widely printed.[9] The hymn is so written that any of these partial presentations makes some sense, since it is everywhere a petition for the same simple total blessing, since stanzas made of independent lines have no dependence on other stanzas, and since the sequence is not argument but action, one action projected with four degrees of intensity. The verses are laid out carefully step by step; any selection of the steps takes us some distance up in the same direction.

A prayer is an effort to bring about what it asks for. A prayer that is prepared ahead of time by a writer for the use of others, operating, so to speak, perpendicular to the transaction of prayer itself, has the rhetorical task of facilitating the working of prayer. Whether or not it presumes to say things so well as to persuade its deity to be favorably disposed, a very suspect role for rhetoric, it may be expected to seek to dispose the petitioners to allow some good to come about, presumably akin to what they are conscious of asking for in raising the prayer. It is not surprising then to find that "Love Divine" offers its congregation an experience in some ways congruent to what it asks for, that is, heaven; and by approximating what it invokes seeks to induce the acceptance of salvation. It defines its God as Love that can dwell in man, and it works by drawing its human congregation into some level of communion transcending self. We will pursue this description further in a moment.

In this view the role of the author is not only to teach but to enable, to arrange the event of singing so that the singers can not only learn about but experience what has been called Wesley's "great tennet, the immediate access of the human soul to the Infinite."[10] The author's task is to calculate and promote the spiritual experience of other people, an undertaking clearly fraught with the possibilities of manipulation and exploitation, akin to the abuses of the pornographer who stages erotic experiences for us.

A doubter may judge the spiritual experience orchestrated by certain hymns to be maudlin, for example, or to pander to racial or national pride, and may question the propriety of any such orchestration. Views similar to these have brought about the exile of all music from some churches, and in the seventeenth and eighteenth centuries were still generating resistance to all hymns but psalms, that is, all texts not taken whole from the Bible. (It may be that Wesley's reliance on biblical phrasing is among other things caution.) Wesley's contemporary Samuel Johnson judged that a poet's words could not promote real religious experience: "Contemplative piety, or the intercourse between God and the human soul, cannot be poetical. Man admitted to implore the mercy of his Creator and plead the merits of his Redeemer is already in a higher state than poetry can confer." [11]

If it is to be allowed that a writer may engage in the art of hymn-writing, and in particular of writing hymns cast in the form of prayer, he must write as a dramatist. He will be writing dialogue, giving all the words to one part, in which the congregation as a whole is cast—not writing soliloquy, but writing the words for one side of the "intercourse of God and the human soul." Doing this properly requires the gift of sympathetic imagination. An admiring scholar says:

> So powerful was the sympathetic link between Charles Wesley and others that it is sometimes exceedingly difficult to be sure whether in his verse he is describing his own experience or identifying himself with that of someone else. . . . He is thinking and feeling himself into the personality of another . . . when he writes for wives and widows, coal-miners and criminals, lay preachers, Loyalist soldiers, or the scholars at Kingswood School. . . . [Such writing] can justly be described as a form of dramatic art. [12]

Wesley wrote, for example, a "Hymn for Condemned Malefactors," of which the second stanza says,

Outcasts of Men, to Thee we fly
  To Thee who wilt the Worst receive,
Forgive and make us fit to die;
  Alas! we are not fit to live.[13]

As dramatist, Wesley wrote in "Love Divine" the script for a progressively rapt acceptance of grace. The script begins with men separated from God and leads up to the ecstasy of the immediate presence of God. The singing congregation knows where it is when it looks up at the beginning to pray that love come down; at the end it imagines, with more or less fervor, being "lost in wonder, love, and praise." Absolute ecstatic lostness in the divine presence is represented. It is mimed by a certain lostness of the singer, which is a religious use of what song makes happen: liberation from the well-defined place and time of the self, into community, concert, communion. In the manuscript of the hymn, Wesley had written the last lines so as to make this connection even clearer: "*Sing* and cast our Crowns before Thee, Lost . . ."[14] Singing now, singing then; to use the words of Keats, "We shall enjoy ourselves here after by having what we called happiness on earth repeated in a finer tone and so repeated."

The words of the song as lesson teach that salvation is not far to seek, that it lies just the other side of acceptance of love and grace, and that such salvation is continuous with heaven itself. The experience of the hymn as sung is to invite the grace that it teaches will save; to pray and praise without ceasing, that is, in the insistent musical present, over which no future different from itself casts a shadow; and to be lost from the world here for the time of the song.

Work Song:
"Blow the Man Down"

Oh, as I was a-rollin' down Great Howard Street,
    Timme <u>way</u>, *hay,* <u>blow</u> *the man down!*
A handsome flash packet I chanct for to meet.
    Ooh! <u>gimme</u> *some time to* <u>blow</u> *the man down!*

This spankin' flash packet she said unto me,
    Timme <u>way</u>, *hay,* <u>blow</u> *the man down!*
There's a dandy full-rigger just ready for sea.
    Ooh! <u>gimme</u> *some time to* <u>blow</u> *the man down!*

This dandy full-rigger to New York was bound,
    Timme <u>way</u>, *hay,* <u>blow</u> *the man down!*
She was very well rigged an' very well found.
    Ooh! <u>gimme</u> *some time to* <u>blow</u> *the man down!*

So I packed up me sea-bag an' signed on that day,
    Timme <u>way</u>, *hay,* <u>blow</u> *the man down!*
An' with this flash packet I spent me half-pay.
    Ooh! <u>gimme</u> *some time to* <u>blow</u> *the man down!*

'Twas when this Blackballer was ready for sea,
    Timme <u>way</u>, *hay,* <u>blow</u> *the man down!*
'Tis then that you'd see such a hell o' a spree.
    Ooh! <u>gimme</u> *some time to* <u>blow</u> *the man down!*

There's tinkers an' tailors an' sogers an' all,
    Timme <u>way</u>, *hay,* <u>blow</u> *the man down!*
All ship as prime seamen aboard the Blackball.
    Ooh! <u>gimme</u> *some time to* <u>blow</u> *the man down!*

Oh, muster ye sogers an' fakirs an' sich,
    Timme <u>way</u>, *hay,* <u>blow</u> *the man down!*
An' hear yer name called by a son-o'-a-bitch.
    Ooh! <u>gimme</u> *some time to* <u>blow</u> *the man down!*

An' when the Blackballer hauls out o' the dock,
  Timme <u>way</u>, *hay,* <u>blow</u> *the man down!*
To see these poor barstards, how on deck they flock.
  Ooh! <u>gimme</u> *some time to* <u>blow</u> *the man down!*

Lay aft here, ye lubbers! Lay aft one an' all,
  Timme <u>way</u>, *hay,* <u>blow</u> *the man down!*
I'll have none o' yer dodges aboard this Blackball!
  Ooh! <u>gimme</u> *some time to* <u>blow</u> *the man down!*

Now see these poor barstards how aloft they will scoot,
  Timme <u>way</u>, *hay,* <u>blow</u> *the man down!*
Assisted along by the toe o' a boot.
  Ooh! <u>gimme</u> *some time to* <u>blow</u> *the man down!*

The second mate stands 'em all up in a row,
  Timme <u>way</u>, *hay,* <u>blow</u> *the man down!*
A seam in the deck he sure makes 'em all toe.
  Ooh! <u>gimme</u> *some time to* <u>blow</u> *the man down!*

It's Fore tawps'l halyards! the mate he will roar,
  Timme <u>way</u>, *hay,* <u>blow</u> *the man down!*
Oh, lay along smartly, ye son-o'-a-whore!
  Ooh! <u>gimme</u> *some time to* <u>blow</u> *the man down!*

It's 'way aloft, lubbers, shake them tawps'ls out,
  Timme <u>way</u>, *hay,* <u>blow</u> *the man down!*
The last man in the riggin' he clouts on the snout.
  Ooh! <u>gimme</u> *some time to* <u>blow</u> *the man down!*

Oh, lay along smartly each lousy recruit,
  Timme <u>way</u>, *hay,* <u>blow</u> *the man down!*
Or 'tis lifted ye'll be by the greaser's sea-boot.
  Ooh! <u>gimme</u> *some time to* <u>blow</u> *the man down!*

'Tis larboard an' starboard on deck ye will sprawl,
  Timme <u>way</u>, hay, <u>blow</u> the man down!
For Kickin' Jack Williams commands this Blackball.
  Ooh! <u>gimme</u> some time to <u>blow</u> the man down!

An' when the Blackballer is leavin' the dock,
  Timme <u>way</u>, hay, <u>blow</u> the man down!
All the pretty young gals on the pierhead do flock.
  Ooh! <u>gimme</u> some time to <u>blow</u> the man down!

An' now when she's leavin' the ol' Merseyside,
  Timme <u>way</u>, hay, <u>blow</u> the man down!
All hands are now ordered to scrub the ship's side.
  Ooh! <u>gimme</u> some time to <u>blow</u> the man down!

An' now when she's clear over ol' Mersey Bar,
  Timme <u>way</u>, hay, <u>blow</u> the man down!
The mate knocks 'em down with a big caps'n-bar.
  Ooh! <u>gimme</u> some time to <u>blow</u> the man down!

An' when the Blackballer hauls clear o' the land,
  Timme <u>way</u>, hay, <u>blow</u> the man down!
The bosun roars out the hoarse words o' command.
  Ooh! <u>gimme</u> some time to <u>blow</u> the man down!

Yes, soon as the packet is well out to sea,
  Timme <u>way</u>, hay, <u>blow</u> the man down!
'Tis cruel, hard treatment o' every degree.
  Ooh! <u>gimme</u> some time to <u>blow</u> the man down!

Ye've handspike hash every day for yer tea,
  Timme <u>way</u>, hay, <u>blow</u> the man down!
An' belayin'-pin soup many times will ye see.
  Ooh! <u>gimme</u> some time to <u>blow</u> the man down!

Now we are sailin' the Western so wide,
  Timme way, hay, blow the man down!
An' the green rollin' seas run along our black side.
  Ooh! gimme some time to blow the man down!

Soon, bully boys, we'll be back round the Rock,
  Timme way, hay, blow the man down!
An' then, bully boys, we'll be snug in the dock.
  Ooh! gimme some time to blow the man down!

An' then all the hands they will bundle ashore,
  Timme way, hay, blow the man down!
To ship in a Blackballer we'll niver do more.
  Ooh! gimme some time to blow the man down!

So I'll give ye a warnin' afore we belay,
  Timme way, hay, blow the man down!
Don't take it for Gospel what spankin' gals say.
  Ooh! gimme some time to blow the man down!

Don't ye go a-strollin' down Great Howard Street,
  Timme way, hay, blow the man down!
Or else such a chowlah ye'll happen to meet.
  Ooh! gimme some time to blow the man down!

For she'll spin ye such lies an' they'll sign ye away
  Timme way, hay, blow the man down!
On a hardcase Blackballer where there's hell every day.
  Ooh! gimme some time to blow the man down!

So we'll blow the man up, bullies, blow the man down,
  Timme way, hay, blow the man down!
Wid a crew o' hard cases from Liverpool town.
  Ooh! gimme some time to blow the man down!

RITISH and American sailors of the nineteenth century sang the chorus of this
shanty in response to a wide variety of
patterns of solo lines, including at least
two Child ballads, "The Farmer's Curst Wife" and "The Twa Cor-
bies." This narrative of the sailing of a packet of the Blackball
line, the first regularly scheduled shipping line in the North Atlantic, is reported from the singing of two sailors, one of whom
had sailed with the line himself in his youth.[1] A written text of any
folk song only exemplifies the song, as it varies from one singing
to another. Work song is even less well represented by a given text
than are other folk songs, because each singing of it times a job
being done by the singers, and the song is cut or stretched to the
occasion. This specimen of "Blow the Man Down" is a relatively
extended one, providing as it would for a hundred and twelve
pulls on a halyard.

Singing at work has been the immemorial recourse of laboring
men and women. Peter Dronke, in a book on the medieval lyric,
quotes a sermon of St. John Chrysostom around the end of the
fourth century:

> Journeymen, driving their yoked oxen in the noonday, often
> sing as they go, making the way less weary by their songs. Not
> only journeymen but wine-growers, treading the winepress, or
> gathering grapes, or dressing the vines, or doing any other
> piece of work, often do it to a song. And the sailors likewise,
> as they pull the oars. Again, women who are weaving, or dis-
> entangling the threads on their spindle, often sing: sometimes
> each of them sings for herself, at other times they all harmo-
> nise a melody together.[2]

Singing to time and to lighten group work is still to be heard in
various places: one author mentions Levantines, Arabs, Malays,

Indians, Tamils, Chinese, Japanese, and Africans, and another various West Indian groups, as now using shantylike songs. The songs now called shanties or chanteys, a name of disputed origin, coordinated manpower aboard sailing ships. They have been traced from scanty records back through late medieval England. (The reference above to sailors singing in early Christian Greece is specifically to rowing songs, on vessels that carried little sail.) They were little in evidence in the eighteenth century, partly because of naval discipline, and came to vigorous, conspicuous life only in the nineteenth. The conditions of work for which they are best fitted arose with the peacetime mercantile sea traffic that boomed after the Napoleonic wars; they declined at the end of the century when shipboard technology changed the work sailors had to do.[3]

"Blow the Man Down" in all its varieties is a fairly specialized shanty. Its anapestic meter, timed to a three-eighths musical measure, marks it as a halyard shanty, used for gang-pulling on the rope that raised a sail. Heaving songs, by way of contrast, used at the capstan, windlass, or pump, timed continuous work, and tend to fall into 4/4 time, a slow march. Among hauling songs, "Blow the Man Down" is likewise distinguishable from shanties that went with lighter tension on the rope—hand-over-hand songs and walkaway songs—and from short-drag halyard songs for raising the smaller and lighter sails highest in the rigging, the topgallants and royals. This song is specifically a shanty for setting the so-called upper topsail, in the middle rank of sails of a full-rigged ship, the largest and heaviest sail that was raised rather than dropped into position. Its spacing of pull-words and its rambling length are adapted to this longest hauling task, hauling the topsail halyard; the halyard passed through a tackle block of several sheaves, which bought mechanical advantage by multiplying the length of rope that had to be pulled.[4]

Along with the clear mechanical function of timing group work that these shanties serve, there is a widely attested feeling among those who have employed such songs that the songs are able to modify hard work in some way for the worker, making it pass more easily. In his book about Texas prison work songs, for example, Bruce Jackson quotes inmates to this effect. One says, "I can do a whole lot more work workin' by time than I can workin' loose. . . . When I sing, picking cotton, before I know anything I be three blocks ahead. . . ." Harold Courlander was told by a Zulu workman in Durban, "If we don't sing we have less breath. Without singing we have no strength," and Courlander quotes similar testimony from workers in Nigeria, Haiti, and Alabama. The sea shanties were regarded as "an extra hand on the rope," not only by the seamen but also by their employers. Frederick Harlow provides the information that "a good chanteyman . . . was often paid more than the common sailor for his ability to get work out of the men."[5] What are the reasons for this inspiriting effect of work songs?

In the first place we may say that the practical effect of synchronizing the efforts of several individual workers happens through a coordinating of their consciousnesses, making a sort of compound workman out of single workmen. Singing together means that attention is focused on what is common and external, the work, rather than what is individual and internal. The rhythm of work is cued by a musical and verbal order given out by the voice of one's own body but tightly governed by assimilation to the pattern shouted out in the voices of the other workers. Feedback between ear and voice makes it very difficult not to be in time with one's neighbors, and the traffic in that circuit makes it very difficult not to have one's full attention on what one is doing.

So much to say that work song prevents distraction. The compound workman works better than a collection of individuals, even if his pace is slow (shantymen could slow the tempo of the work), because his members are none of them half-hearted. They have given up separateness, and as they are free from separateness they are free from the vagaries of the independent mind. They are guarded from wandering in the circles of reverie, from confronting the complaints of their bodies, or from contemplating the work ahead in debilitating discouragement. One of the Texas prisoners says, "When a man get to singing, he doesn't got time to think about his problems or the work." Another says, "Actually we get more work done when there's singing than when we're silent. Because that leads into arguments and confusion if a man hasn't anything to occupy his mind. If his mind is occupied he's steady working in union."[6] Free consciousness can only be less efficient than the occupied mind. We might compare here the speculations of Julian Jaynes, who has argued that individual consciousness is a late development of the last twenty-five hundred years, preceded by the rule of what he calls the bicameral mind that had no access to reflection. Jaynes writes that "fatigue is a product of the subjective conscious mind, and . . . bicameral man, building the pyramids of Egypt . . . with only hand labor, could do so far more easily than could conscious self-reflective men."[7] Distraction, if it is allowed to happen, is alienation from the work at hand. Work of this definitively dull sort can of course be done by a worker with a free mind, and random inspiration might even spur him to extra effort; but such inspiration would be irregular and infrequent. What private inspiration can add is less than what distraction will subtract, and efficiency demands it be damped out. The sea shanty belongs to the age of industrial efficiency within the age of manual work on ships.

From the point of view of the worker, alienation of consciousness from the work at hand presents the danger of despair. Despair of getting through it all not only will lead him to falter at doing the present moment's part, and thus make him inefficient, it will also cause him pain. The device that wards it off is welcome. He does himself a favor by passing the time in song. What is necessary to make time pass quickly was described lucidly by John Locke:

> We have no perception of *Duration*, but by considering the train of *Ideas*, that take their turns in our Understandings. When that succession of *Ideas* ceases, our perception of Duration ceases with it; which every one clearly experiments in himself, whilst he sleeps soundly. . . . And so I doubt not but it would be to a waking Man, if it were possible for him to

keep only one *Idea* in his Mind, without variation, and the
succession of others: And we see, that one who fixes his
Thoughts very intently on one thing . . . whilst he is taken up
in that earnest Contemplation, lets slip out of his Account a
good part of that Duration.[8]

Song can have the function of bridging time by simplifying, re-
stricting, and unifying the ideas in the mind of the worker who
must pass through working time. One of Jackson's informants
says:

> The day wouldn't seem so hard. Even if we did have to stay
> here so long we would soon forget about it and time just pass
> on by like that. That's one way of doin' time.[9]

So the work song confers a benefit on the worker as well as on
the work. To explore further the relationship between worker and
song, we may return to "Blow the Man Down." If we allow that in
this song as in others the words offer a self-of-the-song into which
a singer may invest himself, then the identity that the shanty offers a sailor to put on over his individuality is clear enough: he is
invited to become the compound workman, or, to follow Stan
Hugill in his generic remarks about seamen, Sailor John.

The solo line narrative of this version of the shanty is a sketch
of the myth of Sailor John. Several elements of the myth can be
isolated, although the whole is tightly coherent, in this and in
many other shanties. The principal parts visible in the present
version derive from his attested experience of sex on shore and of
brutal discipline afloat.

The opening stanzas of this text belong to a family of which
the head is the sailor song "Ratcliffe Highway"—not primarily a
shanty, but a so-called "forebitter" for recreational singing—
which recounts a sexual adventure in port, mostly in nautical
metaphor.

Now as I was a-walkin' down the Ratcliffe Highway
A flash lookin' packet I chanc't for to say
Of the port that she hailed from I cannot say much

But by her appearance I took her for Dutch . . .
Her flag was three colors, her masthead was low,
She was round at the counter and bluff at the bow . . .
I tipp'd her me flipper an' took her in tow,
An' yard-arm to yard-arm away we did go,
She then took me up to her lily-white room,
An' there all the evening we drank and we spooned . . .[10]

There is a large repertoire of ingenious and highly unchaste meta-phor used to embroider this basic story, sometimes to the chorus of "Blow the Man Down" and sometimes to other choruses. These stories belong in turn to an extended family of sex-in-port stories set into shanties, which typically begin with the same formula:

As I was a rollin' down the Strand ("Sacramento")

Oh, as I was a walkin' on the quay ("Sacramento")

Oh, as I strolled out one evening ("The Fire Ship")

Jack bein' a sailor, he walked London town ("Bungyreye")

As I walked out one morning fair ("Blow Ye Winds")

As I walked down the Broadway ("Can't Ye Dance the Polka")

As I walked down ol' South Street ("New York Gals")[11]

The same formula is also used elsewhere, as it is in the present text, to begin the story of how the narrator or some other victim came to an undesirable sea berth:

As I walked out one morning down by the Clarence Dock
I heard a bully Irish boy conversing with Tapscott;
Good morning, Mister Tapscott, would ye be arter telling me
If ye've got a ship bound for New York in the state of Amerikee?

Oh, as I was a-rollin down Great Howard Street
I strolled into Paddy West's house . . .

At the Liverpool Docks at the break of the day
I saw a flash packet bound west'ard away

She was bound to the west'ard where the wide waters flow
She's a Liverpool packet, Oh, Lord, let her go.[12]

This last example is of particular interest because it describes an encounter with the "flash packet" at the foot of a Liverpool street, but as an actual ship rather than as a poeticized whore. The two kinds of encounter have much in common.

Sex appears in the life of Sailor John in cycle with his voyages. The circuit is barely interrupted by the shoreline. The voyage pays for sex and drink, and sex and drink make the voyage necessary again. But the phases of life afloat and ashore blur together even more closely than this. The ship as woman ("she's leavin' old Merseyside") leaves him ashore with part of his money, which he spends on the woman as ship; the rest of his money, his advance or half-pay on the next voyage, he can spend on the woman only after committing himself to the next ship, which she is thus eager to have him do.

This spankin' flash packet she said unto me
There's a dandy full-rigger just ready for sea.
So I packed up me sea-bag an' signed on that day
An' with this flash packet I spent me half-pay.

The whore procures him a ship, just as the arrival of the ship procures him the whore: other shanties commonly reverse a stanza in this version, making the flocking of the girls a welcome rather than farewell:

An' now we've arrived at the Bramleymoor Dock
An' all them flash judies on the pierhead do flock.[13]

Reversibility is the key: there are two symmetrical ceremonial moments, when the ship gives the sailors to the concourse of whores, and when the whores give them back. Sailor John's time ashore is like the quick, hot passage of the comet around his sun, which drew him in and launches him out again.

The sexual adventure, which is relatively abbreviated in this version, is recurred to at the close of the shanty in a group of

stanzas widely typical of many shanties in its tone: the narrator
turns his tale to a caution. "So I'll give ye a warnin' . . . Don't ye
go a-strollin' . . . Or else such a chowlah ye'll happen to meet
. . . they'll sign ye away." As prudential moral this would seem to
deny the cycle, to aspire to break out of it. "An' then all the hands
they will bundle ashore, / To ship in a Blackballer we'll niver do
more." But aside from doubts about the efficacy of any good reso-
lutions under such circumstances, song does not easily teach lessons this way—who is lecturing, and who is listening? The rueful
boast of the beginning and likewise of the closing is the voice of
Sailor John, who speaks for the sailor and not to him. Being sadder but wiser is part of the identity of the self-of-the-song. It is not
necessary to call in evidence all the shanties that focus on the
other half of the cycle, the homeward journey and its greedy expectation of the waiting flock, to judge that this knowing testimony about the cycle confirms the cycle. Any stretch of the orbit
implies the rest.

After the shore encounter at the opening of this version, the
solo line narrative is concerned with the initiation into sailorhood
of a motley crew.

There's tinkers an' tailors an' sogers an' all
All ship as prime seamen aboard the Blackball.

Thus introduced in our sixth stanza, they occupy the shantyman
for the following nine stanzas; the girls reappear for one stanza,
and then there is another stretch of five such stanzas. This group
of nine plus five makes so many variations on the theme of lubbers meeting the rough discipline of the ship. Most of them name
the newcomers with derogation or mention violence against them:
"fakirs, poor barstards, lubbers, poor barstards, son-o'-a-whore,
lubbers, lousy recruit; toe o' a boot, clouts on the snout, greaser's
sea boot, on deck ye will sprawl, knocks 'em down, cruel treatment, handspike, belayin' pin." The tone seems to mix contempt,
sympathy, and amusement. The lubbers and their overseers are
both set before us as *seen:*

Now see these poor barstards how aloft they will scoot
Assisted along by the toe o' a boot.

Sailor John identifies himself with neither party. One is a son-o'-a-whore and the other a son-o'-a-bitch. The mates are a common adversary, but here someone else is taking the abuse, a notion not unwelcome to his imagination. The repeated indulgence in describing these scenes of abuse stanza after stanza shows the satisfaction of the initiated at the pains of those now undergoing initiation. A revolving account is being kept in balance: we once suffered through it, but that is somehow justified if others now suffer through it in turn. They are painfully getting to where we are. The place of the old hand is aggrandized the more the severity of the initiation is played up. Our toughness is greater the more we describe the trouble of becoming what we are. In many rites of passage those already initiated inflict the new initiation themselves; and in a sense that is happening here, as the shantyman conjures up scene after scene of misery. He is inflicting the mates on the lubbers. His role as scourge is seen most clearly in the stanzas with implied quotation marks, punctuation that can never be sung, where the words of the ship's officer become without attribution the words of the shantyman:

Lay aft here, ye lubbers! Lay aft one an' all
I'll have none o' yer dodges aboard this Blackball!

With the emphatic assent of chorus to the narrative, the working seamen relive the initiation and confirm themselves in the role of initiate. Like the stanzas about sex ashore, those about the new poor barstards indulge a satisfying sense of being sadder but wiser, fully experienced, knowing.

In this version of the shanty, the solo lines following the extended account of initiation seem to effect a remarkable splicing of mythic and actual, past and present. The initiation has been conjured out of general lore, as something that happens typically or always upon the sailing of a Blackball liner: "When the Blackballer hauls out o' the dock, To see these poor barstards . . ."

Now the point of view changes. The shantyman modulates in the last of the initiation stanzas into the second person, "Ye've hand-spike hash every day for yer tea"; and in his next stanza into the first person plural, "Now we are sailin' the Western so wide." The voyage of the lubbers, once they suffer their initiation, becomes this voyage. The initiation leads to us, in the present, and helps construct the image of who Sailor John is. Does it follow that the shanty is a document of real sailing on the Blackballer, sung only or properly about the middle of an Atlantic crossing of this kind of ship? Probably not: we know at least that some versions of the shanty name ports that the actual Blackball line never served, so the shanty must have continued to function when there was considerable distance between the voyage described and the voyage on which it was employed.[14] What is apparently assimilation of the mythic voyage to the real one is better seen the other way around, as reference from whatever shipboard moment is present up to the mythic voyage of the tough, experienced Packet Rat, Sailor John.

In the final stanza solo line and chorus come together.

So we'll blow the man up, bullies, blow the man down,
  Timme way, *hay,* blow *the man down!*
Wid a crew o' hard cases from Liverpool town.
  Ooh! gimme *some time to* blow *the man down!*

The shantyman joins his mates by echoing the chorus they have been answering him with and declares their identity as the true packet rats he has been singing about. For the last time, most explicitly, he confers on the men at the rope their participation in the legend, and they give their last affirmation in chorus. Some attention should be paid to the words that they have been using in their responses. The solo lines give the identity of the true Blackball sailor discursively. The chorus lines are the verbal acts that share breath and energy with the exertion of work. If it is true that the shanty invites its singers to escape from individuality to a common identity, these participatory words of the chorus are the true lines for the part. They support and affirm what the shantyman says, by completing his musical pattern. What do they say in making the affirmation?

To consider first the most conspicuous word, "Blow" means at least in origin "knock": "Knock the man down." Hugill quotes from Cecil Sharp's collection of 1914 a version that has "knock" for "blow"; it is still sung in the West Indies by whalers:

I hit him a lick and I fetch him a kick
And a yea, yea, blow de man down
Blow de man down in de hol' below
'Low me some time to blow de man down.

Doerflinger reports that "packet sailors called the second and third mates 'blowers and strikers'—the two terms meant the same thing."[15] As imperative or declaration of intention, the phrase "Blow the man down" lets out under the license of song the aggressive reaction of the sailor subject to the blowers and strikers. As the verb is one of the pull-words each time it is used, there is in the first place a neat transference of the aggression into useful labor. But this understanding will be modified below.

The contraction "Timme" is more or less the same as "Gimme," although the two are not used in parallel here, and I am not sure that the latter was used to start choruses. Variations are used in many choruses: "To me" or "To my" in the shanties "Hooker John" and "Stormalong," and "Tibby" in one version of "We'll Ranzo Way" are other forms.[16] The place it fills in the line is the unstressed cue before the first pull, a place also filled sometimes by such words as "then," "and," or "so." Though it seems always to be transcribed as part of the chorus, some performers recreating shanties give it to the shantyman rather than the group, demanding their response. In any case it leads the first pull-word of this chorus, the heart of the chorus and the most common pull-word in shanty singing, *'way*, for *away*:

Lowlands, Lowlands, away, my John

To me way you Stormalong

Away Santiana!

'Way-ay, heave away! ("Bay of Mexico")

Away for Rio!

Timme way, hay ho high ho ("A Long Time Ago")

and so on through the repertoire.[17]

In notes on a "hooraw chorus" shanty, Hugill comments that the "Way hay" is a transcriber's rationalization, "being nothing more than a savage yell hard to put in print."[18] But as such it is an assimilation to the articulate word *away* in more sedate choruses like "Away for Rio" or "Lowlands away." Pull-words vary across a frontier of intelligibility, being sometimes close to the sing-out that probably is the earliest form of shanty. As mere "savage yell" for one great effort, that most primitive vocalization-with-work does not have the group-timing or time-managing functions of sustained work song. Perhaps it came into existence because rising to exertion beyond normal routine is helped by or requires or leads to breaking past normal vocal decorum. A worker plays at being wild in speech and releases uninhibited effort; he frees his facial muscles for fierce contortion, which are normally under the restraint of looking human. In a highly evolved shanty like "Blow the Man Down" the crying-out has settled down to a level of articulation where it must either flee semantic reference—"High diddle dee, high diddle bum"[19]—or have a little of it (though semantic content will be diminished by the hypnotic repetition). At this level the sense of *away* corresponds to the acceleration from rest of a burst of muscular effort, moving something that is not easy to move; and also, as suggested by the "bound away" choruses, the exhilaration of willing, and being in, motion, outward or homeward, away from the barren present. "Gimme" in "Gimme some time" is the remaining pull-word, and is here not a place-filler; it participates in the transfer to work effort of aggression against "the man," as if pulling the rope bought the chance to strike back.

There is a final point to be made about this transfer. We have said that sea shanties flourished in the period of industrial efficiency within the sailing era. Work song more generally seems to be promoted by the adversarial relationship of overseers to the working gang. (A prominent exception is the use of shanties for communal housemoving in the West Indies.) In his careful discussion of the work songs of black convicts in Texas, Jackson suggests a possible function of such songs in the prison environment:

> The songs change the nature of the work by putting the work into the worker's framework rather than the guards'. By incorporating the work with their song, by, in effect, co-opting something they are forced to do anyway, they make it *theirs* in a way it otherwise is not. [20]

The meaning of displacement of reaction from one object to another is that the two objects are both the same and different, and either likeness or difference may be emphasized. We may say that in singing "Blow the man down" the sailors let out aggression toward their bosses, or we may look at it the other way and say that their behavior in doing so is precisely not an aggressive reaction to repression but rather disciplined compliance in doing what they have to do. Pulling the rope is so unlike punching the mate that it is hard to judge whether the will to do the latter spurs on the former. Jackson's hypothesis illuminates the judgment and by focusing on the value of the work for the worker, suggests the complexity of the transformation. I think a further, perhaps quite small, modification should be made of Jackson's idea.

Under the gun or belaying pin of the overseer the working gang sings their own song, their own verbal possession, affirming their own views, lore, and collective self-image. As their own spoken things accompany the labor, their exertion becomes emphatic declaration of the speech. Body movement becomes the emphatic gesture appropriated to the words, and the work gets done incidentally. It seems to me, then, that it is not so much a matter of making the work their own; the work gets as little attention as it can survive on. It is irredeemably the property of the bosses and the system, defined by the working environment that is not made by or for the worker. What is made the worker's own is his effort. His alienation from the work is prescribed by the situation as soon as he looks at it with his own free personal eyes. His effort might likewise be alienated from him, taken rather than given, in slavery. Song makes possible a powerful, convincing assertion (it makes itself true) that the effort by which the work is privileged to get done is the worker's own.

Such an effect goes beyond mere displacement of the reactive energy from anger at the boss to savage pulls on the rope. Something affirmative has come into being. Perhaps sublimation is the right term for what happens, or that term may also be too simple. The substance of it is that song makes possible an escape from the frustrating standoff of worker against boss, in which the worker owes and pays one way or the other. In escaping from the single resentful consciousness of the coerced agent, he participates in a free giving away of willed effort that is really his own. He makes the expressive gesture that fulfills the identity he has taken on.

Popular Song: "After the Ball"

A little maiden climbed an old man's knee
Begged for a story—"Do Uncle please."
Why are you single; why live alone?
Have you no babies; have you no home?
"I had a sweetheart, years, years ago;
Where she is now pet, you will soon know.
List to the story, I'll tell it all,
I believed her faithless after the ball.

After the ball is over, after the break of morn—
After the dancers' leaving; after the stars are gone;
Many a heart is aching, if you could read them all;
Many the hopes that have vanished after the ball.

Bright lights were flashing in the grand ball-room,
Softly the music, playing sweet tunes.
There came my sweetheart, my love, my own—
'I wish some water; leave me alone.'
When I returned dear there stood a man,
Kissing my sweet heart as lovers can.
Down fell the glass pet, broken, that's all,
Just as my heart was after the ball,

After the ball is over, after the break of morn—
After the dancers' leaving; after the stars are gone;
Many a heart is aching, if you could read them all;
Many the hopes that have vanished after the ball.

Long years have passed child, I've never wed,
True to my lost love, though she is dead.
She tried to tell me, tried to explain;
I would not listen, pleadings were vain,
One day a letter came from that man,
He was her brother—the letter ran.
That's why I'm lonely, no home at all;
I broke her heart pet, after the ball.

After the ball is over, after the break of morn—
After the dancers' leaving; after the stars are gone;
Many a heart is aching, if you could read them all;
Many the hopes that have vanished after the ball.

"FTER THE BALL" was the first song to become a popular hit in the modern sense of the word. In 1892 and succeeding years it sold five million copies of sheet music, and eventually perhaps ten million. No earlier song had achieved anything like this level of commercial success. Stephen Foster's songs, written two generations earlier and better known today, had early sales of only about fifty thousand, or one percent of those of "After the Ball."[1] The institutions of public entertainment in America were coming together into a big business—a bit later than oil, a bit ahead of the automobile—with the evolution of mass production and mass marketing. The sheet music business was evolving alongside an industry that placed pianos, harmoniums, and player pianos in middle-class homes, in the decades before the First World War; it would be outgrown in the twenties and thirties by a successor industry of records, record players, radios, and movies.

Late in the nineteenth century successful sales of a song came through performance by popular singers in touring musical shows, after which members of the audience might buy the sheet music— and then their friends, and then others who learned the song was fashionable, and then others who happened across it in music stores just because many copies were in those stores. Success could breed further success; but in retrospect from the age of mass media promotion, it is difficult to see how this relatively contingent sequence could lead to the remarkable popularity achieved by "After the Ball." Other songs subsequently reached similar heights: between 1900 and 1910 nearly a hundred songs had sheet music sales of one million apiece.[2] But the success of "After the Ball" is still a landmark. It pleased the public faster and more widely than any promotion, or "plugging," as it was soon to be called, could have contrived. Charles K. Harris, the young man who wrote it, was unknown either popularly or professionally outside Milwaukee. When the song had set him up in business in New York with money, reputation, business contacts, and experience, he spent a career trying in vain to duplicate his sudden first success. The song belongs in the class of spontaneous public favorites with the *Beggar's Opera*, *Pickwick Papers*, and *Birth of a Nation*. It met an extraordinary readiness in the American public of its day to indulge in the sentiment it expressed.

When a work of narrative fiction or drama captures a large public, it generally offers a protagonist whose course of adventures carries members of that public to a symbolic resolution for certain conflicted ideas and feelings that they share. A popular song can do this work only in a very telescoped fashion. Because a song is, in comparison to narrative and dramatic forms, not dynamic—not serial, progressive, articulated—the participation in a song by its audience is not so much a matter of psychodynamics, we have said, as of psychostatics. Song, even narrative song, tends toward tableau. It presents a constructed mood or pose, and if such a mood or pose is predicated of some character distinct from one's ordinary self, an identification figure, that figure will be a protagonist without an agon. He will be *situated* somehow with respect to a past or a surrounding present. In "After the Ball" this situating of the hero is helpfully explicit: the uncle spends the whole song in a chair. (Songs may be built on a series of tableaus rather than on one, but to the extent that song becomes narrative of events, the "protagonist" figure becomes object of attention rather than assumed identity, and the point of view offered by the song retreats from that of character to that of storyteller.)

In a sense extended beyond his physical posture, the situation of the hero of "After the Ball" is one its audience found very affecting. It is one of three elements that must have built up together the great and wide impact the song had, the others being the proposition offered in the lines of the chorus and the music to which the song and especially its chorus were set. The music had considerable merit, and the song's fortunes were much advanced by frequent instrumental performances given it by John Philip Sousa's band at the Chicago World's Fair in 1893. Tune and bits of verse of the chorus are lodged obscurely in many memories even now, especially the first seven or thirteen notes and the first five or seven words ("After the . . . dah dee dah"). For study of those and the rest of the words of the song, it is useful to notice that the music is a waltz: it has the sound of the music at a ball. The words of the chorus, the other separable element of the song, make a commentary on the situation of the hero. We will return to them after considering what that situation is.

Shrewd guessing could supply nearly all of the hero's extended situation from the song's rather unmetrical first line, "A little maiden climbed an old man's knee." The line gives a male and female, intimately close and also definitively set apart from each other. Even before the song called him her uncle we would know that they have neither the intimacy of man and woman nor that of parent and child which attests previous intimacy of man and woman. Assuming we are embarked on a love song, there are two directions this very chaste encounter can take: the song can attend to the child, and offer a recursion into childhood love, as Harris did in his song "Let's Kiss and Make Up"; or it can turn to the mature adult and explain what barriers to sexual and parental relationships are implied by his dandling someone else's little girl. This latter is what the song does: it asks and answers the question, "Why are you single; why live alone?"

The situation is loneliness. So described, the song belongs to the main line of popular song, much of which in many styles has made a great anatomy of loneliness. Harris gives his hero loneliness with a specific history to rationalize it, and consequently the song gives its audience a specifically rationalized loneliness for their indulgence: to enter into the song is to place self within the myth to explain a felt lonely state. The myth, the story in the second and third stanzas, is easily recognizable as the property of the English and American Victorian culture from which it comes. It is the substance of innumerable melodramas and sentimental novels. In its song form here, condensed and poised in a few bare lines, and those attested as a valid form of the myth by very unusual popularity, it presents an especially ready occasion for analysis, not to say diagnosis, of the meaning of that story.

Analysis of popular song as fantasy must be content with some kinds of vagueness. "After the Ball" is presumptively the fantasy of millions of Americans, and then again properly of no one; it would even be unfair to attach it too deeply to Harris, who after all made it to sell. No doubt (but we can never be sure) it was moving to some people, as answering their own deep feelings; and lightly appealing to others; and only froth on the music to many others. The proportions of these groups cannot be known at this distance of time, nor their makeup by age or sex. While they bought this song in relative preference to thousands of other songs, there is no security in claiming any specific primacy for it among fantasies of the time, many of which were surely not for sale in comparable form.

These limits suggest that interpretation should not be highly specific and exclusive, because a large audience will have had a range of responses and found a variety of gratifications, and that no chain of deduction should trace very distinct, essentially individual psychological structures around the common myth. This said, consider a range of meanings this story may be thought to have:

1. It is a fantasy of being free from family obligations—of decorous but unencumbered bachelorhood.

2. It is a fantasy of a safe, reclusive retrospect on the excitement and troubles of life, but of having experienced them intensely.

3. It is a fantasy of having been loved. Since the woman's rejection by him is followed by nothing else we know of her but her

death, one can easily suppose that her broken heart killed her, so it is also a fantasy of having been died for. (Compare Gretta in Joyce's *The Dead*—"So she had had that romance in her life: a man had died for her sake.") The self-validation implied, to the contradiction of any present absence of admirers, is considerable.

4. It is a fantasy of being dreadfully guilty of this unfortunate death, of carrying a mild form of the gothic wanderer's curse: "That's why I'm lonely, no home at all."

5. It is a fantasy of having been sinned against. The unfaithfulness is rationalized away after it had shattered him, so imputation of inadequacy on his part is removed, while the dignity remains of having been victimized by fate.

A further series of possibilities draws on two useful devices deriving from Freudian dream analysis. In story analysis intriguing patterns appear if we consider, first, that all events in such stories be understood as willed to happen by the protagonist; and second, that more than one figure may stand for one referent, or one figure have more than one reference (splitting and condensation).[3] Under these rules, we the protagonist may have fantasized

a) punitive death fulfilling a grudge against women in general, or against one who would venture to trifle with me, or partiers and indulgers in balls; or against my first lover who insisted on kissing another man—that is, my mother. (In Harris's song "'Mid the Green Fields of Virginia Far Away" a man recalls that his mother's heart broke when he left home.) One function of the story is to tell "Where she is now," that is, where she has been put, and the answer is in her grave.

b) exchange of the kissing-prone sweetheart for the niece-child, or change of adult woman into child-woman, presumably easier to dominate or escape from.

c) hesitant rejection of sex. The hero may be considered split between two figures, one of whom takes the privilege after the ball of "kissing my sweetheart as lovers can," and the other, aghast at the prospect, who drops and shatters the offering to her that is also both hearts and withdraws into celibacy. The one who kisses is then professed to have been doing so in a brotherly, chaste manner, which is not what it looked like at the time: this version of the fantasy does include some will toward sex, but overcomes it.

Finally, the fantasy history may be generally described as one of surviving, of outliving whom and what one loves, and of having grown old.

In this range of possible meanings to this public fantasy— there may be other quite different meanings—there is some central, common import. The issue raised is isolation, whether willed or not, succeeding to shared love or the possibility of it, and confirmed by death. The role of death is more important than its parenthetical mention in the song indicates. Permanence is the essence of the state of things brought about by what happened. Death has a central place in the sentimental myth system that the song represents: the idea of death in itself, the threat of death, the untimeliness of death, has more weight in melodrama than in tragedy. The poignancy of a Victorian sentimental vignette turns on the interruption of expectations and relationships by death, whereas the tragic vision seeks the meaningful pattern that death closes. *In Memoriam* may stand for the view of death that must be defined here: it is an appalled vision of unfulfilled possibilities and bereaved survivors. Homelier examples are furnished by other songs written by Harris. In "For Old Time's Sake" a runaway sweetheart is rediscovered, only to be lost to death; in "Break the News to Mother" the young soldier dies as he is reunited with his father (Harris's account was, "How to end the song with a punch puzzled me. While still in the barber's chair a thought came to my mind in a flash, and I cried out, 'I have it! I'm going to kill him!'"); in "Always in the Way" a little orphan girl seeks an explanation for the loss of her mother; in "Hello, Central, Give Me Heaven," she tries to call her on the telephone; in "While the Dance Goes On," it is the child who dies while the mother is away; and so on through several more.[4] Although these songs had more modest success than "After the Ball," Harris mined them from the same vein, where death breaks into a family, a love, or a friendship, to take someone away and to leave someone behind fixed in loneliness.

Another comparative example may help show the character of the fantasy of lonely survival in "After the Ball." The tableau of the song is strongly reminiscent of the American best-seller *Reveries of a Bachelor* by "Ik Marvel" (Donald Grant Mitchell), which was published in 1863, sold a million copies in its authorized edition, and was pirated some fifty times.[5] Mitchell's bachelor is twenty-six, a fairly early season of world-weariness—his youth reminds us that Harris's "old man" is young enough to have a small niece, old strictly in the sense of living on lamely beyond his possibilities of loving. Mitchell's bachelor does for himself what the buyers of Harris's song paid for, he works up imaginations of various romantic and familial scenarios terminated by untimely death:

> The coal slips down below the third bar, with a rumbling sound,—like that of coarse gravel falling into a new-dug grave.
> —She is gone!

> Poor little Paul!—he has sunk under the murderous eddies of the brook!

> Bella—sweet Bella was dead! It seemed as if with her, half the world were dead. . . . I walked out into the air, and stood under the trees where we had played together with poor Tray—where Tray lay buried.[6]

Mitchell is ironically forthright about the appeal of reverie: "Can any wife be prettier than an after-dinner fancy, idle and yet vivid, can paint for you? Can any children make less noise, than the little rosy-cheeked ones, who have no existence except in the *omnium gatherum* of your own brain? . . . I wonder . . . if a married man with his sentiment made actual, is after all, as happy as

we poor fellows, in our dreams?"[7] But praise of the power of fancy
to deliver a golden world stops short of explaining why the fantasies end in separation by death. (The *Reveries* first appeared in
the *Southern Literary Messenger*, which also printed Poe's stories,
which likewise generally deal with the mortal subtraction of
someone close to the narrator.) We can see some clarification in
the copresence in *Reveries of a Bachelor* of imagined bereavement
and snug contentment. The setting at the start of the book is heavily emphatic of his self-sufficiency. The sought-out reveries of loss
somehow comfort and confirm singleness.

> But the toils of life are upon me. Private griefs do not break
> the force, and the weight of the great—Present. A life—at
> best the half of it, is before me. It is to be wrought out with
> nerve and work.[8]

This return to the world has a certain zest to it.

"After the Ball" does not seem to have zest, except in the lilt-
ing waltz of the music, but the note in the analogous *Reveries* is a
clue to the nature of such fantasies of survival, and that is that
they imply competitiveness. The loneliness that is referred to survival beyond peers, including lovers, belongs to an individualis-
tic, competitive society, to the society that produced the *Origin of
Species* as well as *In Memoriam*. To be a lonely survivor is another
way to experience success. Although the uncle's station in life is
not known, the similar reverist in "'Mid the Green Fields of Virginia" is "living in a mansion grand." Retrospect, however sad,
on those who have dropped away is hard to separate from complacency at winning through to the great Present; whichever side of
the coin one is looking at, the coin belongs to the economy of
competition.

After the Ball is the title Harris used for his own autobiogra-
phy as well as for the uncle's similarly retrospective reverie, and
it provides examples of several kinds of the competitive preoccupation with who survives whom. Late in the book he devotes
seven pages to a listing of firms that entered the music publishing
business and went under while his own flourished. He records an

argument with George M. Cohan about what sort of songs would "outlast" what other sort.[9] A dozen times or more he returns to reflections on what has become of his early peers.

> Horowitz, who dreamed of following in the footsteps of Booth and McCullough, is now writing short sketches for vaudeville. . . . Fisher . . . drifted into the newspaper field. . . . John W. Nau died ten years ago. . . . Mathews, owing to serious illness, retired from the stage about twenty years ago, and has since passed away. . . . Both Hallen and Hart have passed to the great beyond. . . . Paul has been dead many years. . . . A few years ago [Tearer the Great] was burned to death, together with his performing lions, in London.[10]

Two curious personal anecdotes both bring together the elements of intimacy, competitiveness, and mortality. The first, beginning in the language of emulation ("leading"), tells of friendly rivalry and suggests a murderous edge suppressed under sentimental affection for the departed friend:

> I certainly enjoyed myself at the West End Hotel, then one of the leading hotels in Long Branch, especially as Pete Dailey, who was the leading comedian . . . was among its guests. . . . Every morning at breakfast Pete would say: "Have you heard [word of a hoped-for success]? Any wires or cables?" I was compelled to smile, my reply always being: "No, Pete, not yet, but soon." The laugh was soon to be on Pete. . . . I rushed over to Pete's room. He was shaving at the time. I ran in and slapped him on the back, yelling like a Comanche Indian, "Who's loony now?" and flashing the cablegram before his eyes. Poor Pete almost slashed his throat in the excitement. "Read it, you old pessimist!" I cried. His eyes were dim and his voice husky as he turned to me and said: "Charles, honestly I congratulate you from the bottom of my heart." Dear old Pete, how I loved and admired him.[11]

The second anecdote incorporates (if the word is nearly a pun, it is used in Harris's own account) competitive professionalism, fascination with death, and rejection of sexuality—the description of the Tombstone Club in Milwaukee he helped found and decorate.

> We arranged to cover the walls with white canvas and then procured the services of scenic painters from various theatres to paint the walls with graveyard scenes, skeletons—everything as weird as possible. A long table was built in the shape of a coffin. The top of the table at which the president sat would lift up to disclose the wax figure of a male, donated by a member, in full evening dress. . . . At the lower end of the table was a skull attached to a wire which extended to the president's chair. When this wire was jerked, the skull would open, showing the interior filled with smokes. . . . One of the Club's inflexible rules was that no woman should ever cross its threshold. [12]

Daniel Walker Howe, in a survey of the main elements of American Victorian culture, observes that "a well-known Victorian value was competitiveness, an attitude reflecting the excitement and sense of power with which they faced the world," and he traces its manifestations beyond the economic system to party politics, denominationalism in religion, "emulation" in education, and "intra-personal competition" as ethics. [13] The pervasive mode of competitiveness lies also behind the sentimentalism that presents itself as maudlin and morbid, because the fascination in such sentimentalism is not only with dying and disappearing out of the world but equally with surviving beyond the disappearance of others. To put it another way, the culture of "After the Ball" is fascinated with the question of what competing possibilities come to be fulfilled and with unfulfilled possibilities: it contributes every entry under "might-have-been" in *Bartlett's Familiar Quotations*. [14] The characteristic reverie answering to fascination with competition and differential survival is the survivor's retrospect out of loneliness.

"After the Ball" is not competitive in its fantasy content, except as it recalls a gesture of prickly jealousy. The connection between sentimental loneliness and competition may be clearer in the lines of the song's chorus. The commentary that the chorus offers on the uncle's story is generalization:

After the ball is over; after the break of morn—
After the dancers' leaving; after the stars are gone;
Many a heart is aching, if you could read them all;
Many the hopes that have vanished after the ball.

There is foreboding in these waltzing lines. They prophesy desolation as the common lot when the promises and anticipations from the time of merrymaking come due in real life. The ball is a formal but hollow ritual of social, participatory good feeling. Ballroom dancing is cooperative; waltzing to the music lifts one out of self. People behave as if loving partnership were the rule of life, and then when daybreak comes many of them, more than one thinks, will be lonely instead. Their hearts will ache specifically for what, at the ball, they pretended they had, which was an escape from individual self in love and dance.

The main lines of the fantasy of rationalized loneliness that the song made available to its public are a sketch of the general lot in the culture in which the song itself competed and won out. "After the Ball" was the fanfare for the age of big-business popular music. It helped to build the Tin Pan Alley where promoters jostled to score a hit. It signalled that the intensely competitive ethos of American culture was ready to make Horatio Alger heroes out of songwriters, so that even the relaxations and recreations of the country were evolving a high-pressure competitiveness. The appeal of the song, most generally, must have been that it lamented the loneliness of this world, as much of both the popular and the high art of the age did. Offering, as a song can, a waltzing participation in chorus, alternating with the brooding loneliness of the uncle who had not trusted love, it has the effect of testifying that the lost, outlived vision of shared love would be a better choice.

10

Jingle: "Pepsi-Cola hits the spot"

T O A TWENTIETH-CENTURY American the street ballad considered in chapter 5 carries overtones of other daily experiences besides those of sensational journalism to which we connected it. The song has much in common with the familiar boosting of consumer goods sung at us over radio and television: it is, in effect, a singing commercial for the whale. As a song exercise contrived for profit by one party for a second party, such a sold ballad has two collateral lines of descent in the modern marketplace. One is popular song, which sells directly whatever experience it offers in itself. The other is sung advertising, which is given away freely (insistently) to sell something else associated with the experience it provides.

The range of states of mind and heart sold now by the popular music industry takes in some species of boasting and marveling not too alien to that implied in the whale ballad. Phallic boasting is obviously part of the first-person strut that first became noticeable in white popular music with Elvis Presley but that has an honorable longer history in black performance and recording. Songs about more or less mythic heroes also sell wonderment ("Big John," "Bad, Bad Leroy Brown," "Ballad of the Green Berets"). Some songs have won wide popularity by displaying prodigious events, like "The Wreck of the Edmund Fitzgerald."[1] The consumer is usually given such a song free at first, over the radio, like the Londoner hearing his ballad first from the singing balladseller, and then pays for the recording so that he can replay at will whatever plays out in the song—the music, and also (in these cases) the chance to marvel.

In the most general terms, advertising song also relies on the consumer's readiness, even to the point of parting with money, to participate in attesting to marvels. The common content of all ad-

174

vertisements is that the given product or service is better than whatever presumes to compete with it. This pseudoinformation might be taken for merely conveyed information, as advertising must generally pretend that it is; but of course advertising is essentially rhetorical, concerned with transmitting the message in such a way as to induce acceptance of the message. The problem of the advertiser, then, is to seem only to be having his say to me, while really doing or saying something that will make his say into my say. I must be persuaded that his version of the world of bread or automobiles is the true version, so that I will attest to it in my behavior. If his message is that his particular product or service excels others, and his goal is to dispose me to adopt as my own view the view that it excels, it must be generally the case that he wishes me to enter into a marveling and even boasting attitude with respect to his product.

The principal mode in which this aim is pursued, of making his boast into my boast, is testimony. The testimonial commercial aims to be vicarious. When an athlete tells the television audience about the virtues of a car rental service, the advertiser has procured this admiring testimony to be delivered by a figure with whom much of the audience somehow or sometimes identifies: spectator sports are nothing if not vicarious. Movie and television stars are likewise nothing if not stand-ins for ourselves, and their testimony is correspondingly valuable to advertisers. The most common endorser of all, the anonymous actress playing the housewife, is exactly the viewer's self as she wishes to be seen from the outside. When my stand-in tells the camera about rental cars, the significant transaction is not that he tells me but rather that I, by proxy, tell the world.

The utility of song in this promotional context stems from the inherent tendency in song experience for the listener to assume the perspective implied by the words. A successful singing commercial works like a successful testimonial commercial to put us in the place of attesting. What we have just noticed about spoken testimonial shows that song is not the only medium for this importation of sentiments into our consciousness. Most communication to us that feels satisfactory, that is not accompanied by a defensive discounting, achieves the status of what we accept, and in hearing or even reading it we participate in the communication. We admit it into consciousness and thereby admit it to have some validity.

The defensive discount is weaker as our capacity to identify with the source of the words is greater. Words in voice promote the identification more readily than words written. Printed advertising copy, with the exception of that pursuing certain special effects such as authoritativeness, runs naturally to the colloquial, to the speechlike—heavy, for example, with sentence fragments. With the beginning of radio in the nineteen-twenties and the flowering of television at mid-century, commercial persuaders were given immensely increased access to citizens' consciousness. A speaking voice for advertisers was of such value, and the addition of a speaking image to facilitate the self-projection of the consumer was such a grand bonus, that the commercial advertisers undertook and have sustained the sponsorship of the entire American broadcast culture.

The first commercial messages brought into homes by radio in the early twenties were formal and impersonal, but within that decade advertisers began to exploit the mechanism of identification natural to the medium. Performers made familiar by their radio programs were called on to deliver the messages; dramatizations drew listeners into personal situations of appreciation for products; and in 1929 a barbershop quartet in Minneapolis sang the first broadcast jingle, for Wheaties.[2] Ten years later, over network radio, jingle first reached the level of national saturation that has since been available to it. The first massively promoted singing commercial was

Pepsi-Cola hits the spot,
Twelve full ounces, that's a lot,
Twice as much for a nickel, too
Pepsi-Cola is the drink for you!

It was played 296,426 times over 469 stations in 1941, and more than a million times by 1944, becoming in effect a new kind of golden disc hit, a recording sold a million times by broadcasting to advertisers. Its enormous success, reflected in its entry into playground folklore in a variety of parody forms, has been a signal ever since of what such jingles can achieve in making advertising copy intimate to the public.[3]

The testimony on behalf of the product offered in such a jingle as this is different from spoken advertising testimony because of the nature of song. Jingle cannot have or even seem to have the discursive content of a talking commercial. Whatever one thinks of the information conveyed in a talking commercial script, some large part of what is brought over by such talk inheres in the discursive form itself, the impression being given that the product will sustain serious talk about it. Singing commercial sacrifices this appearance of rational discussability of the product. It also sacrifices a certain claim to responsibility, a sense that the words can be traced back to their source and that "you can take it from me." There is no apparent personal source of sung words. Spoken testimony comes from the pulpit or the witness chair, but sung witness is something that even the original, broadcasting performers seem merely to be joining in on.

The peculiar properties of song make both the strength and the limitations of jingle compared with other tactics of advertising—for example, compared to the common practice of accompanying a spoken or visual message with instrumental mood music. Mood music can establish an association of the product with a feeling state; jingle can attach words to the state. Because the words are sung words, they will to some extent be experienced as the subject's own words, the more so the more effective the jingle.

The words are appropriated in this way when the commercial is heard, and consequently certain qualities attach to them when they are recalled. It is not exactly that they return as words one once uttered oneself. They are present in the mind as public words, verbal property not bearing the sign of ownership by someone else. Heard sung, they achieved the air of what we and the singer or singers joined in on, rather than of what so-and-so said. Recalled, they come in assembled jingling lines as common property objects, available to pass through inner or outer speech and so pass as one's own. The state of existence as unappropriated property is reflected in the availability of successful jingles for verbal play by children.

Such a state is close to the standing in the memory of proverb. Proverb is what every slogan aspires to become, but to describe the condition fairly easily arrived at by song as proverblike does not necessarily imply easy success for song in motivating sales. Jingle has not driven out other tricks of marketing, and like other tricks it is subject to debate over its effectiveness.[4] The relationship of lines of words preserved in memory to any behavior at all is problematical.

If jingle words are like proverbs, it might seem that they would have better access to the will than is allowed them here: that they might be consulted in conscious choices. It may be suspected however that proverbs share the impotence of songs, rather than that songs partake of any supposed influence of proverbs. For one thing there are the pairs of contradictory proverbs, as of commercials, current in the same culture and advising opposite courses: "Look before you leap"; but "He who hesitates is lost." When both are available to consciousness, which will guide choice? Surely neither guides choice very often. What either can do is to confirm choice. Proverbs are solicited, like solicited advice, to confirm and support the choice of what one is otherwise inclined to do. Jingle words may very well appear in the mind on the occasion of a buying choice, as well as at other annoying times on the cue of verbal association, but they can seldom bring even pseudoinformation to bear on decision itself. At such a time they chorus reassurance about the choice just made.

The makers of advertisements have come to realize that jingles do little simple delivery of messages. One advertising executive was quoted in the *New York Times* as saying, "The days of merely rhyming a lot of product attributes are gone, or almost gone." A writer of jingles adds, "The point of jingles is the same as the point of popular music; finding a hook that is repeated and that the listener can't get away from."[5] The idea of implanting hooked words in the mind, rather than true or false information, acknowledges the listener's tendency to take possession of suitably formed phrases and snatches of song and calculates that the hook can be attached to a string held by the merchant.

In popular songwriting the "hook" expression has long been used for the striking, catching turn of musical and verbal phrase that the writer hopes will attach itself to the listener, but there is an important difference in the two implied uses of this hook. The hook of popular song works to snag the listener into the song itself; purchase of the recorded song may naturally follow as a concrete taking possession of the song already held in the mind. The hooked sample attaches itself to us for its own sake. It is self-referring: the hook curves back on itself. Self-reference is often visible in the verbal form of such a hook, returning upon itself as paradox, or as repetitive regression, or as absurd phrase refusing to connect to expected context: consider, among the first-place successes of one year, 1973, where hook happens to coincide with title, "I Love You Love Me Love"; "Skweeze Me, Pleeze Me"; "Can the Can"; "12th of Never"; "Rubber Bullets."[6]

Advertising hook, on the other hand, aims not only to lodge in the mind but then also to pull buyers toward products. The crucial extra function is, as we have said, problematical; it must rely on semantic reference of the hooked words back along the attached line, and this reference is in conflict with the self-reference that lodges the hook. A well-made slogan or song hook is like a proverb in this as well. It will often show in its form the kind of recurved self-reference visible in many proverbs, like Benjamin Franklin's "Haste makes waste" or "Where there's marriage without love, there will be love without marriage": compare "When you're out of Schlitz, you're out of beer"; "When you say Budweiser, you've said it all"; "The one beer to have when you're having more than one"; "If you've got the time, we've got the beer."

The listener takes possession of such phrase-objects, and they take possession of him. The hook does draw us into the experience of jingle as song. No doubt that experience can associate good feelings with the sponsoring product, apart from or in addition to those of music alone; but direct payoff is doubtful. Being in the song is something the mind inclines toward, and the entry into commercial song can be more easily precipitated than exploited. Geoffrey Leech, in a study of British advertising, has observed that much advertising copy is dense with the kind of pattern noticed here in hooked jingles (where there is always, of course, the superimposed pattern of music, often similarly hooked), and that

> such density of schemes and repetitions is not uncommon in traditional ballads and modern popular songs. But perhaps a more fitting analogy, bringing out the ritualistic aspect of advertising jingles, is with children's games and nursery rhymes.[7]

Professor Leech does not carry his suggestion further, but it seems helpfully suggestive in the present context. A chance to play these musical games is something that the buyer of recorded popular song pays for. The advertiser has reason to hope to tax this same delight in song games by using it against resistance to the buying of his product. The obstacle to his hope is that when we enter into jingles we may well not be listening to what the mind's voice is singing. Song is not always heard distinctly from the inside; following the curves of the jingle will not necessarily point us to the product. Even when we are annoyed with jingles, what they draw the mind into is play.

11

Record: "White Christmas"

"PRILL" in Spenser's *Shepheardes Calender* presents Hobbinoll lamenting to Thenot that the boy he loves is lovesick for a girl. The boy, Colin, has given up piping and singing, at which he was very skillful. Thenot urges Hobbinoll to sing one of Colin's songs, and Hobbinoll obliges with an elaborate lay in praise of Elisa, queen of shepherds. Thenot's words to persuade Hobbinoll to sing are these:

But if hys ditties bene so trimly dight,
I pray thee Hobbinoll, recorde some one. . . .

This old sense of *record* reflects the origin of the word in *cor*, "heart," the place of memory: "to produce (something) known by heart." Related senses included "to get (something) by heart so as to be able to reproduce it," which survives in the word applied to the practicing young birds do, quietly, before they become proficient adult singers.

Spenser's pastorals belong to the tradition in which literate poets imagine their preliterate predecessors. What is projected here onto Colin and Hobbinoll is not only Spenser's supremely literate "song" to his queen, but a literate idea of recording and reproducing, or as books now say in their copyright notices, of information storage and retrieval. The "trimly dight" effusion of Colin's is presented by Hobbinoll with an implied guarantee of fidelity. Colin's song is separable from Colin; in the world of pastoral it need not be written down to be preserved for reproduction, because it is secure in the heart of Hobbinoll, his personal rhapsode. Outside that special world, such faithful memorizing implies writing down first, rendering into a document, which early became the principal sense in English of *record*, both noun and verb.

The idea of records is the idea of keeping something that is threatened with being swept away, the idea of not forgetting. It has to do with marking a reference point in the extension of time, with a view to mastering that time and staking it out like a territory. It is not the same as literacy, since record is not necessarily written. It can be carved, drawn, or tied in the knotted strings of Inca quipu. It can be oral, though not when it has the textuality of Spenserian verse. Literacy does mark a great accession of recording, the qualitative change in what Carl Sagan has called extrasomatic information storage. In English society, the comings of Calvinism and capitalism seem to have introduced new kinds of record-consciousness, in the journals and ledgers of the new middle class. Ian Watt showed that the evolution in the seventeenth century of ideas of individualism, individual experience, originality, and unique fact fostered the rise of the novel as the new literary form of the eighteenth century. The novel is a model record of life at a level of detail not seen before.[1] As Watt shows, Defoe's *Robinson Crusoe* makes an excellent exhibit of these tendencies, as Crusoe the castaway records from day to day his food, his work, his spiritual insights, and his score against the cannibals.

This last instance is enough like a sporting encounter to recall the innovations of the twentieth century in record-keeping, as in the statistics of sports. Sports apparently have given us a sense of *record* now very common, "the superlative instance." Daily papers commonly give us such an item as one from the time of this writing, headed "Snake Sitter Breaks Record": "I have had a black mamba slither over my face in the dark," the man is reported as saying, "but I think the challenge has been worth it. My name will be entered in the Guinness Book of Records."[2] Part of the meaning of such curiosities is that they are actions undertaken for the sake of the record of those actions. The root idea remains the same, however, as it is in the whole realm of record: one places something, in this case one's self, upon record in one's anxiety that it may be lost in time and change. It answers the reigning preoccupations about these matters for the reporter to add, in the case cited, that the previous record-holder died in a traffic accident shortly after his achievement.

We have seen in the discussion of ballads that the possibility of placing a song on record, that is, of writing it down, changed the nature of song from creative recomposition to artifact; and in the discussion of street ballad, that song as artifact became naturally an article in commerce. In a higher cultural sphere Spenser's "song" to Elisa, if we compare it to what it playfully pretends to be, shows us a parallel difference. Rather than an occasion of homage, a tributary performance, an event, it has in Spenser's book the nature of part of his record, an achieved work of art, and inevitably part of a commerce of political favor and literary repute.

Hobbinoll *records* his friend's song and thus attests, confirms, and enjoys his possession of the song, text and tune, in his own heart. Spenser records the poem on paper and gives the text to every reader; if there were really a tune, he could have recorded that as well. The writer of songs has had this power of conferring on readers, through the technology of printing, the instructions for making the living song for himself. The surpassing of this technology was promised by Edison's invention in 1877 of a device to record the human voice itself. In the succeeding century the technology of recording, together with that of broadcasting, has given us as our most common experience of music the recorded performance of song. Not merely the song, but the singing of it, is now the article of a massive commerce.

The meaning of these records and this commerce is in some ways illuminated by the other uses of the word *record*. We can begin to explore these connections by consulting the *Guinness Book of World Records*:

The greatest seller of any record to date is *White Christmas* by Irving Berlin (born Israel Bailin, at Tyumen, Russia, May 11, 1888), with 25,000,000 for the Crosby single (recorded May 29, 1942) and more than 100,000,000 in other versions.[3]

The gratification offered readers by such an entry as this must derive in part from the competitive excitement implied by every instance of winning. As we have noted in consideration of "After the Ball," such competitiveness has been the hallmark of modern popular music. It has even become overtly part of the entertainment the industry provides. No other industry, surely, employs for sales purposes, to induce consumer interest, the statistics of which hundred of its ephemeral products have sold most successfully in a given week. The glamour of the "charts" is a curious fact, far outdoing that of best-seller lists in book publishing, though it may have closer analogues in sport or in the stock market.

With some exceptions phonograph records are not obviously made to preserve the performance event from oblivion, though of course they have that function for music historians and hobbyists. They are made to be sold, and as such their music has something in common with snake-sitting as activity undertaken for the sake of the record of it. This commercial purpose of the makers does not, however, exhaust the meaning of these records in our culture, the ways in which they manifest the idea of *record*. To see this meaning more fully, consider now the record recorded in *Guinness*, Bing Crosby's recording of Irving Berlin's "White Christmas."

For commercial-legal reasons it is not possible to print here the text of "White Christmas" as has been done with the songs considered earlier in this study. We will undertake to discuss the song as it may be hoped it is recorded in the heart of the reader: its words, its music, and the voice in which it has principally been experienced. In any case, much of what will be said here may be understood and judged without reference to the details of the song.

Consider first the most ghostly aspect of this intangible internal song, the quality of the voice singing it. Bing Crosby's voice, or more precisely his use of his voice, responds to a highly significant development in electronic technology, the evolution about

1925 of carbon-microphone recording apparatus.[4] Crosby was not quite the first but he was the most successful and influential practitioner of an art directly traceable to that technical innovation, the art of crooning. Any time before 1925 an entertainer singing softly could only be giving an essentially private performance. Neither singing from stages nor singing into the morning-glory horns of the earlier recording industry could be done softly. Henry Pleasants, a historian and analyst of both classical and popular singers, says, "Bing's most original contribution was the lowering of the voice, not so much in pitch as in intensity, to a conversational level." He quotes the critic Peter Reilly: "After the advent of Crosby, pop singers stopped singing *at* you, like Jolson, and began singing *to* you, like Bing."[5]

The stressed prepositions in this last statement recall, and challenge, the argument advanced in the introduction of this book that song in general seems to speak *for* us. The relationship of the listener to the singer is a crucial issue in the consideration of "White Christmas," and here as elsewhere it can be affirmed that listener merges self into singer. Crosby and his fellow radio and film singing idols have, indeed, been easily recognized to be significant identification figures, for-singers, for their audiences. Pleasants remarks of Crosby, "The manner in which he has sustained, for his generation, the image of its youth may well account for the extraordinary longevity of his hold upon the affections of an enormous public."[6]

The voice for us in Crosby's case is an intimate, private-sounding, confiding voice. The "in-the-room intimacy," as one critic described it,[7] of Crosby's voice exploited a new mode of song. The importance of such intimacy in broadening the range of feeling states accessible in popular music can be seen in the fact that this intimacy made possible by the microphone is not restricted in its exploitation to soft songs. Even loud rock performances make use of the intimate hand-held microphone to keep voice present to the listener amid any amount of accompanying sound.

The easy softness of Crosby's voice in the "White Christmas"

recording is appropriated to reverie. There are many other possibilities, more than can be invoked by naming them, but including urbane sensuality, amused affection, and wry regret. The
breadth of alternatives is useful to remember since the utter appropriateness of this voice to this song seems fated or typed but is
really art. The mood of the song is declaredly, by its first words,
dreaming, quiet holiday daydreaming, and Crosby's reverie voice
embodies—implies the embodiment of—ease, warmth, quiet,
languor, dreaminess.

The voice records a text. Since the main concern throughout
this book has been the place of words within the phenomena of
song, songs in which words have a certain prominence have been
examined. Again, then, it must be remembered that the place of
words in songs is a matter of more and less. In classical singing
and in jazz singing, notably, the voice may often be more a musical instrument than a medium of language. Pleasants argues that
American popular music has been built on a return to a prominence of language in song similar to the place given language at
an early stage of the European classical tradition.

> What distinguishes the popular singer most fundamentally
> from the classical singer is, in my opinion, the relationship of
> his singing to language.

> Where the popular singer comes closer than the classical
> singer to the earliest Italian models is in his acceptance of
> song as a lyrical extension of speech. He is more concerned
> than is the classical singer with text, both with its meaning
> and with the melodic and rhythmic manner in which it might
> be spoken. One popular singer praising another is likely to
> refer to his "reading of the text, or lyric." It is not a formu-
> lation I have ever heard . . . from the mouth of a classical
> singer.[8]

Pleasants traces this orientation of popular music toward speech
back to two principal sources: the recurring infusion of black stylistic influences, which have made all styles of American popular

music to some extent Afro-American; and the coming of micro-phone technology.[9]

The text of "White Christmas" registered in American hearts has a relatively strong, central participation in the experience and memory of the total Crosby-voiced song. It constitutes more of the song than the texts of other songs may: more, for example, than would be the case in a song by Louis Armstrong, whose musical presence overwhelms his texts, which are treated with detached amusement. But not unreasonably or unrepresentatively more. The larger concern of this discussion with what is typical in modern recorded songs can, I think, be usefully pursued in this particularly clear example. Popular song is text-intensive.

The song describes a holiday reverie and in doing so declares and performs such a reverie. Like the *reverdie* "Sumer is icumen in," "White Christmas" offers participation in a song-experience appropriate to a certain common occasion, not so much about the occasion as licensed by it. The words specify certain qualities to the reverie. They turn it away from whatever is present in order to evoke white Christmas from the past and invoke it upon the future—they do not describe it as present. They sketch the meaning of white Christmas in the images they associate with it.

In the first place white Christmas is a timeless constant. To say that it is a faithful recurrence is not quite strong enough, because that would be to speak the language of changing life. Ordinary Christmas comes around every year and passes for a day. White Christmas is a stop. Consider the stasis of the tableau. Not even sound, which takes time, intrudes: the image is of children (seen and not heard: this is specifically an adult reverie) in the pose of listening in case the sound of sleighbells should come. Their verb is parallel to the verb of what snow does lying on the treetops, of being rather than doing, despite the superficially active sense of the words. The tableau is surprisingly close to that in another of Crosby's greatest hits and this country's favorite Christmas songs, "Silent Night," with the difference of transposition to sacred holiday:

Silent night, holy night
All is calm, all is bright. . . .[10]

"White Christmas" makes no reference beyond the word "Christmas" to any religious symbol or aspect of the holiday. Its reference is to the natural season of snow; but again, that season is only the associative context for a still image, a pause out of time. The dreaming posited in the first line is properly drowsing-dreaming, the so-called hypnagogic still-image dreaming of the lightest stage of sleep, as opposed to the eye-moving action dreams of deep sleep or the active fantasies of waking.[11]

The ending of the lyric is a secular benediction invoking stability. The easily benign, indiscriminate good wish for the future, expressed wonderfully in Crosby's warm and assuring voice, is not in the nature of real wish, defined by doubt of the event and hence anxiety, or of prediction. It is evidence, rather, of the timelessness of this very moment of mood evoked and conferred in the song. It has absolutely no relation to future, or to real past (that is, particular memory). It is an instance of the delicate, noncommittal construction called by the grammarian George O. Curme the "sanguine subjunctive of wish." As such it is of the essence of song. With a superficial suggestion of communicative and even performative power, it really contemplates neither real future Christmases nor real persons to enjoy them. The syntax preceding the benediction is ambiguous—as we replay the song in memory we discover that the phrase about Christmas cards might go grammatically either with what comes before or after it—but the main sense given if we reconnect these semiautonomous lines is that the benediction is bestowed a bit absently on anyone the reverist writes a Christmas card to, and they have nothing to do with us.

The reverie is solitary as well as still. No one is addressed: no ghost of a listener is part of the ostensible shaping occasion. Props, of the insubstantial sort evoked by song, are very spare. By inference the Christmas cards are present, so by inference there is an indoor set, warmth, perhaps semidarkness, perhaps a window with no snow beyond it. Inference is not particularly at work for most listeners; this song does little to stimulate it. "White Christmas" invites us into the place where the reverist is only to invite us beyond it, into his generalized, composite memories that ours may assimilate to. The solitary, private but not particularized excursion into stylized memories is notably unsocial. Nobody in particular, no single person even as fictional representative for possible classes of figures in memory, is referred to. The benediction is in the second person, but it will be mailed.

The turn inward that the song describes and promotes suggests the general nature of the myth of a white Christmas. Snow that falls and lies undisturbed is proof that ordinary movement and business are suspended. Nature encourages and reflects the pause from doing that is part of all holidays but especially of the one associated with the cold longest nighttime of the year, and with warm indoor cosiness, especially for the snow countries of Europe and North America. White Christmas is abstention from activity. It blankets differences of place and differences made by time. It blurs thoughts; it blurs differential memories and differential human relationships, as white contains and blurs all colors. It damps movement and discursive thought, and it sinks toward sleep. Compare its religious analogue:

Silent night, holy night
All is calm, all is bright
Round yon Virgin, mother and child
Holy infant so tender and mild
Sleep in heavenly peace
Sleep in heavenly peace.

It is interesting to note that like "White Christmas," these lines are syntactically ambiguous. That such universally familiar lines should be so awkward to make into normal sentences is strong testimony of the autonomy of song lines. One effect here is that, like a good bedtime story, the stanza concludes in a lingering gentle imperative urging sleep, not very clearly appropriated to the child in the previous lines.[12]

Although "Silent Night" is similar enough to "White Christmas" to help show the rightness of reverie for the Christmas occasion and the naturalness of song in connection with such reverie, not all of our Christmas songs fit this mold. According to the researches of Joseph Murrells, the second most successful copyrighted song in history is "Rudolph the Red-Nosed Reindeer," which has likewise accumulated massive seasonal sales since it was introduced by Gene Autry in 1949.[13] It is hard to see much in common with the magic stillness of "White Christmas" in this success story of the can-do reindeer, which is in fact a reasonably close analogue of "The Bitter Withy," the scorned child vindicated. It has to do with a very different side of Christmas, a social and civil preoccupation with encouraging self-esteem in children and making the sleigh run on time. "Rudolph" does have one intriguing link, however, to an earlier stage of this discussion of record, namely, the kind of success Rudolph achieves. When his performance compels love from the scoffers, they tell him that he will go down in history.

There is some small connection between this promise and the fact that it has been fulfilled. There is some connection between the briefly surfacing fantasy of going into the permanent record and the fact that Americans have taken the song into their hearts for at least three decades of history. Rudolph's reward as the song describes it probably has little directly to do with the appeal of his song; it is only that there is a clue in that reward of how it is that massive popularity of records may be understood. Consider first the case of such seasonal songs as have been discussed here. We will then consider the more general case of all popular records.

It seems likely that what is called "classic" status for a holiday song is itself a major factor in continuing sales at successive Christmas seasons. In the twentieth century the circumstances of holiday celebration have changed drastically from one generation to another for most American families. Places of residence and styles of living shift so fast that nostalgia for whatever can be taken to be traditional is urgent to most people at Christmas, and it has dictated the strategy of a great deal of retail business for the season, including the entertainment business. Besides the two best-selling songs noted so far, three others are included among the most successful popular songs ever (again the rankings are from Murrells in 1974): "Winter Wonderland" (3), "Little Drummer Boy" (6), and "I Saw Mommy Kissing Santa Claus" (15). No tabulation is available for aggregate sales of the public-domain Christmas carols that are clearly in the same class with these songs for recorded sales—we have noted the success of Crosby's "Silent Night." The season is freighted with the sense of a need to hold on to something unchanging in a world changing very fast.

If, by whatever aptness, some symbol such as Rudolph, the Little Drummer Boy, or Frosty the Snowman can become a big seasonal hit once, the holiday urge to remember will give that commercial property a chance for indefinite renewal of some part of that popularity. Beyond these conspicuous accretions to popular Christmas stock, much of the rest of holiday entertainment business is likewise a return to whatever seems traditional, rendered by whoever the new makers and performers happen to be. In the styles and with the personalities of whatever is modish in a given year, there will be a renewal of what we had last year, what we seem to remember from childhood, or what we suppose our forebears enjoyed.

For the record business this sentiment means considerable trade every year. For the buyer of a Christmas record it means the satisfaction of having the familiar music on command for the occasion when that mood is called for. Having the song in his heart firmly enough, he can put on the Christmas music and suffuse some actual span of time with what he accepts to be timeless Christmas. No doubt this music is most commonly a very casual background to other things, activity of some sort. Still it is a link of whatever is going forward with the past, specifically because they both participate in what seems timeless, and that is a solid good for which people pay money year after year. The meaning of having a Christmas record is an instance of the central meaning of record: it is a hedge against time.

In this light the idea of buying and having any recorded song at all can be seen to have similar content. It is of the nature of song in general to stand still. Song turns away from linear process and gives participation in a standing pattern. A recorded song is a grasped chance for the owner-listener to seem to escape from time, or to escape from seeming to be bound to linear time, depending on which perspective one takes to be finally more valid.

The popular song industry appears to be a theater of delirious change. "Fashion" names only the long-period waves in a very ripply surface. Competing performers undergo continual stylistic evolutions of their own in pursuit of the elusive formula of hit. Yet perhaps it will not seem paradoxical to say that the more things in this welter change the more they stay the same. The barrage of newest sounds, latest hits, is clearly enough a hectic effort in the industry to find something that duplicates what was found to be successful last time. For the buyer-listener it is also a continual effort to find something nearly constant dressed in its latest dress. This pattern of continual return can be described in a variety of ways, on several scales.

In a historical view there is a significant pattern of recurrence in American popular music.[14] We have cited the conclusion of Pleasants that American pop is by its essence an Afro-American music throughout its history, a conclusion shared by other analysts. Beginning with minstrel shows and Stephen Foster, through ragtime, jazz, swing, rock, and disco, one generation after another of the predominantly white audience has responded to the fresh instance of a primary American encounter of European with African. When one stage of the music no longer seemed vital with the energy of that encounter, there has always been a latest sound that again seemed to defy what had become too established and to renew the discovery. In the broadest terms this pattern suggests that what seemed new and right to a given generation of the audience has had in it each time a significant common factor with what had seemed right before, which is identifiable as African-derived freedom from rhythmic, melodic, and various other constraints inherited in the tradition of European music. The quality flavoring the song performances embraced by the public one decade after another has changed less than it seems to have changed when any given generation looks back.

On a finer time scale, the careers of writers and of performers often appear to show rapid change. Any writer or singer who enjoys continuing success is likely to show more or less stylistic evolution. Sometimes that evolution may include basic change in kinds of song, but a great deal of it can nevertheless be seen as the writer's or performer's struggle to remain for his audience what in his first successful efforts he was discovered to represent to them. Especially in the current era of long-playing records and tapes where a purchaser typically buys about a dozen songs at once, knowing perhaps one of them from radio display, most such purchases must be considered purchases of the voice of an artist or group (or, of course, the instrumental sound) as opposed to transactions to acquire the songs themselves. This blind, or deaf, purchasing would be less the accepted routine than it is if buyers were often much disappointed. In fact they know well enough what they are buying in a new set of songs: it will be new instances from the range of what the known artist offers them in songs. Artists and writers often, in fact usually, seek to modify what they produce so as to render it gradually effective to a broader and broader audience; but cases must be rare of any change that willfully renounces any audience at all. What is from one angle the exploration of new territory, then, is from another angle an effort to run fast enough to stay in place. One of Bob Dylan's commentators asserted that it is the effort of meeting this greedy demand of the public for twelve songs a season that is referred to in Dylan's image of strapping on the heart-attack machine. From the audience's point of view the demand is what is expressed in one of Steve Goodman's songs:

Give me some words I can dance to
And a melody that rhymes.[15]

What is called for is new songs in new modes, certainly, but still songs in which we can easily do the mental steps of an old familiar dance.

The flood of new songs offered to the public, the buying of the latest records in such staggering numbers, cannot be understood simply as a fast voyage through new realms of experience. Part of the truth is that we are buying the closest equivalents we can find of the songs that worked best for us last week, last year, or long ago. It is no mere derogation of the quality of this music to say that in an important sense our favorite songs are being written over and over again. Unsympathetic outsiders will readily agree that all the songs of some group or some style sound alike, but depreciatory reduction is not what is argued here. All opera also sounds alike to the uninitiated. The challenge to the creative artist, writer, or performer of popular music is to find the new way to strike the pose, set the mood, be the identification model for what is already in the possession of his or her public.

A few other signs of this deep pattern of recurrence may be noted briefly. The definition of a hit is that it is a recent song that we now want to hear regularly. The radio stations will program very little time for first-play records. Their listeners do not want much novelty, even of the generally consistent current production of would-be hits. I have heard one station manager say recently that his policy is to give listeners the impression that they will hear their favorite songs every time they tune in. Such intensity of exposure saturates and fatigues the fan's response to any hit fairly quickly. After the lapse of some time it may return as a veteran ex-hit; some programming seeks specifically to ferret out such golden memories old enough to be not merely unfashionable. Likewise there is a steady though small proportion of new record production that is the rerecording of old songs. There is an occasional overt effort to revive an entire style.

The dynamic, in summary, seems to be that an artist generates personal versions of some of the songs of the day. The listener samples the artist's work on radio in the chinks between already familiar versions that have already become hits. Liking it, the listener gives money to be able to have and to hold the performance-song, and in the case of album sales, ten or so sister songs as well. If the artist is very talented, he will find new ways to continue to be the same Bing Crosby, Elvis Presley, Carole King, Stevie Wonder, or Rolling Stones (sometimes the "same" group even when personnel change), despite the inevitable fading of the charm of any single performance, however perfect. The fan will buy the latest record and then the successive latest record to have the power to seize each performance while it is the performance of mode, and to be able to command its recurrence. He will pit these songs on the record against the flow of time until other records push into its place. The two ideas are united in the idea of record, and also in the idea of song: there is the hurry of change, and there is the profound desire to deny it. There seems to be a continual passing away of every experience, and there seems to be the chance in every song to be free of it. Dancing to this music and these words, the dancer becomes the dance, and the dance is not something that changes. Our new records becoming old are our symbols of the unresolvable dualism. As objects keeping the record of songs through time, they are the correlatives of what we hold out from time: intervals where we think we see that the isolating differences of the world of extension and duration are not the whole story.

Conclusion

First Born, the grandfathers told, had emerged from quivering mud to the rhythm of his own heart and so man had known the true rhythm from the beginning. Soon afterwards man had learned to use this rhythm for making songs. And then certain ones had discovered the true power in song, the power for making spiritual contact.

—Ruth Beebe Hill, *Hanta Yo*

IT MAY BE that we can begin to experience song before we are born. If so, song is the only form of art and perhaps the only expression of what is specifically human that can reach us in the womb. The unborn child, with developed sensory apparatus after the seventh month from conception, has little to sense in weightless darkness except sound. His ears are plugged, but it has been established that he hears some kinds of sharp stimuli from the outside, and so he might hear sounds made within his mother's body as well. Curiously, the limiting factor is not his hearing or even the insulation of the mother's body but the deafening roar of the mother's circulatory system, which has been figured to sustain a noise level of almost ninety-five decibels, about the level found on a subway platform. Still, the sound of the vocal cords is loud throughout the body, as a stethoscope shows, and the mother's intermittent voice may be a perceptible feature of that internal environment. Language, articulated into the air by our lips, tongue, and teeth, is not propagated backwards into the body, but the voice box sound that powers speech hums, with the amplitude and frequency modulations that shape the outline of what is heard outside as speech. The newborn in the suddenly quiet outside world learns quickly, within a week, to tell the mother's voice from other voices, and he may be helped by a long familiarity with the timbre of her speech.[1]

The child knows, in any case, the rhythm kept by the mother's heart, a rhythm that remains soothing after birth. (Dr. Lee Salk argues that the comforting familiarity of heart sound is what has taught mothers to prefer to carry infants in their left arms, a preference visible for example in paintings of madonna and child.)[2] If the unborn child also knows the mother's voice, he does not "know" it in distinction from other voices, inaudible to him, or as the property of his mother as a person, since he does not know about persons or know his mother distinct from himself. The voice of the mother is simply part of existence. The changing tonal outline of her talking vibrates around and in him in vague patterns of human expression. Its rhythms and contours of pitch are partway between what we hear as speech and what we think of as music. Sometimes, however, the mother may actually sing, adjusting her voice to steady rhythm and tune, and the casual and transient patterning of speech be replaced by wordless vocal music. Then existence becomes a song.

More mothers undoubtedly sing to their infant children after those children are born than sing during pregnancy. A child restless in the frustrations of becoming a separate individual is very commonly soothed by singing. The voice of the mother, who is now a separate person, occasionally guilty of absence, shares its singing with the listening child and lulls the child out of worry about the time and space that may loom between want and gratification.

The words that mothers sing to their children dismay the humane critic. Falling cradle and all from the top of a tree is only the most well known of the discomfitures that lullabies wish sweetly on children they are putting to sleep. Lullabies are best understood as work songs for mothers. A mother who sings some of the comically mean things in lullabies resembles a captive laborer venting spleen at the taskmaster:

I'd hang all mates an' skippers
I'd hang 'em by their flippers. . . .

Siembamba, Mama's baby
Twist his neck and hit him on the head
Throw him in the ditch
And then he will be dead.[3]

Lullabies speak for mothers, or for whoever else has to rock the cradle, rather than speaking to the baby. The baby is generally addressed, with promises, threats, or reassurances, but the crucial thing is that it does not matter at all what one tells the baby because the baby does not understand the words.

The baby more or less does understand the lullaby, however. If a dangerously provoked adult were to menace an infant and really mean his threats, surely the infant would cry rather than settling to sleep. The child understands well enough that the mother, father, brother or sister who is willing to sit by and enter into a lullaby is committed, for the timeless present of a song, to keeping up the role of bed-sitting, cradle-rocking presence. The lullaby words may express that role in various ways: by assuring of the quiet security of the environment, which projects the lulling-situation outward on the household and the world; by wishing fabulous rewards on the child (if only he will sleep); by offering teasing threats that attest, with exasperation, to the adult's condition of servitude; or sometimes by very explicit soliloquy. A folklorist says, "There are . . . many sad little lullabies complaining of the mother's weariness and hard lot, of the father's absence, neglect, or drunkenness. A Basque song says that papa will surely come home drunk from the tavern."[4] The mother, or some surrogate, is fully present. In singing a lullaby she declares and enacts, like the sailor at the rope, her role, her mothering presence.

The baby accepts it. The baby's experience of the mother's song is more than response to music in itself and more than response to the mother's ordinary speaking voice. In singing, whatever version of motherhood the words express, the mother's voice is especially motherly. Separation, which is only coming to be established as the order of the child's life, is suspended. The mother having entered into her song, the child enters it too, they are fully together, anxiety is irrelevant, and sleep is easy.

Early and basic in many persons' knowledge of song, then, is what is to them nonsense song. Nonsense song is also what much of children's own singing is even when they are old enough to hear semantic meaning, and it is valued as play—"Mairsey doats and doasey doats"—along with songs like the perverted Pepsi-Cola jingle that play with meaning. For adults as well, some songs are still enjoyed as nonsense or at least without sense, including art songs in languages not understood. The affects of voice contribute some proportion of what has been studied and analyzed in the chapters of this book as put into music by language.

The study of living cultures has suggested that song became part of human life at a very ancient time, probably first as nonsense song. The roots of song go so deeply into the origins of human society that some scholars ("Did the Australopithecines Sing?") have suggested that early man could sing before he could talk. There has been song, in any case, at least for most of the time there has been language. Bowra, in his survey and analysis of the anthropological literature, finds only a single South American tribe not possessing song in our usual meaning of the word—articulated language set to patterns of vocal tones. Song with words has been for almost all cultures a vital bridge between what passes in separate lives and what endures in community experience. Song is familiar poetry, family and community poetry, the poetry of common experience.[5]

The ancient history of song is probably nothing against it with most people, but the fact that it is so early and intimate in personal history raises the question whether the enjoyment of song is generally or necessarily somehow regressive. Some of the studies in this book find hints of indulgence in the childish or infantile in the texts of songs. The holly and ivy carol seems to invite it, and Campion's pastoral idyll embodies a trace of regret for having been weaned. Beyond explicit notice already taken of such tendencies, there is more in the descriptions we have given of various song experiences that might invite such interpretation. The lostness-in-love hymned and promoted by Wesley's church song would, on a Freudian reading, be a clear exhibit of the "oceanic feeling" that Freud, in *Civilization and Its Discontents*, found in religion and referred to the time of infancy, before ego differentiation. Furthermore, the general case of song experience characterized in the introduction and echoed throughout the present book is continuous enough with that description of hymn to associate most songs under the same diagnosis. Indeed, writers about song from Athanasius to Zuckerkandl have agreed in noticing an aspect to it of self-escape and communion.

It has been argued that all aesthetic experiences, and many other experiences as well, partake of an element of return to the infantile. Norman Holland has developed this idea carefully and fully. Though he does not discuss song, he begins his study of literary response with the idea of absorption into art experience in terms that would clearly embrace the song-experiences we have examined. Along the way he assembles a variety of quotations to witness that many arts have been described as absorbing the reader's or viewer's separate self into something else. Tyrone Guthrie, for example, wrote that the theatrical director must "interest the members of an audience so intensely that they are rapt, taken 'out' of themselves," and added, "You can be absorbed listening to music . . . by a great painting . . . even . . . in a philosophical argument"; Bernard Berenson said that in visual arts, the spectator "ceases to be his ordinary self. . . . Time and space are abolished and the spectator is possessed by one awareness." A moviegoer reported that "in the cinema I dissolve into all things and beings."[6]

Holland argues that "this experience of total absorption is far more typical of entertainments than of masterpieces," and that in such experience people "lose track of the boundaries between themselves and the work of art." When this happens, he says,

> we have partially returned to that original "all-embracing" feeling before the ego "separates off an external world from itself."

> Our ego boundaries between self and not-self, inner and outer, become blurred as we approach, in part, the undifferentiated state of earliest infancy.[7]

Both the observations of Holland's witnesses and his analysis seem relevant to the understanding of song. We will consider first one and then the other.

There is a clear kinship of the various aesthetic experiences that makes us forget selves, obliterate our attention to where we are in time and space, and draw us towards unity with the other. When Keats was touching up his early *Endymion* he hit on a notion of how such experiences can be analytically arranged, which he called, in a letter to his publisher, "a kind of Pleasure Thermometer": first comes the sensuous delight in natural beauty ("a rose leaf"), then delight in art, specifically music.

> *Feel we these things?—that moment have we stept*
> *Into a sort of oneness, and our state*
> *Is like a floating spirit's. But there are*
> *Richer entanglements, enthralments far*
> *More self-destroying, . . .*
> *[leading up to] love and friendship. . . .*[8]

Without attempting to graduate the thermometer more finely, to place song a little higher or lower than play, movie, novel, or painting, I would like to hazard briefly in this conclusion a few comparative suggestions.

As an aesthetic entanglement song may be more like the visual arts than it is like other verbal arts. Visual entertainments, as we now see clearly in the case of television, can have a nearly hypnotic, immediate power to absorb the viewer, proportional to how visual data bulk large in our normal sensory relations with the world. Words lag in comparison, and words by themselves lag behind song. It is easy to see that advertisers have grasped these relative priorities. Written copy is rigorously subordinated to graphic visual display whenever both are present. When the medium is sound, in radio advertising, mere words call as often as possible, or affordable, on musical accompaniment.

Absorbing the customer is what advertisers want to do. They are investing well in choosing visual displays of all kinds, and then song. Correlatively, the quickness and thoroughness of our absorption in nonadvertising entertainments or art is orderable in this same way, visual first, and then, among things heard, song first. This ordering means that the ordinary experience of song is perhaps less quickly and fully absorbing than a glimpse of television, but more so than a bit of speech or print. Along one axis, "absorptiveness," song lies a bit beyond most verbal artifice and on the way to the visual.

There is another important dimension to consider in placing song among other experiences: into what do we enter? In the statement of Tyrone Guthrie quoted by Holland, Guthrie goes on to say, "You may say that if [the audience of drama] are taken 'out' of themselves, then they must be taken 'into' something else, and, logically, that 'something else' is the imaginary world of the play." Visual representations take us, allowing whatever partial reservation, into some particular illusion. Likewise, on the other side of song, verbal absorbers of various kinds take us into particular narratives, dramas, dialogues, monologues. This is less the case with song than with other verbal arts and perhaps less than with representational visual arts. Song in this view is more like abstract painting or abstract sculpture than like anything that particularizes an illusion.

Of course there are particulars to the tableaus of song, and much of the discussion in this book has been devoted to them. But to compare song for the moment only to the other verbal arts, no other thing that we do with words has such an insistent sensuous overlay, or better, such a peremptory subordination to an external aesthetic form as does song in having a tune. What the words of a song are saying has everything to do with our culture, our taste, and our occasions, but that verbal content does not detain us so much as do the scenarios of more illusive art. We enter them, we pass beyond them, we have "stept / Into a sort of oneness," and that relatively routinely, easily, quickly, as our aesthetic experiences go.

What then of the psychoanalytic interpretation of this passing over into oneness, as a (perhaps constructive and healthful) regression into infancy? However song may be like or different from other things that absorb us, could not song experience be described as Holland describes reading experiences, as "partial return" rather than as "self-escape" or "self-transcendence"? Some readers will prefer such a description. The mechanism Holland describes is on its own terms quite persuasive, and persuades at least me of a connection between profoundly felt aesthetic experiences and certain barely recoverable experiences of early childhood. As the essays in this book will have made clear, I have preferred to try to understand these experiences as analogous each to the other, rather than only the later ones remembering the earlier. Wordsworth's ode on this subject states this alternative view. His childhood memories included "obstinate questionings / Of sense and outward things," by which he explained that he meant a sense of spiritual unity, in which he was "unable to think of external things as having external existence . . . I communed with all that I saw as something not apart from, but inherent in, my own immaterial nature." Recollected later in life, these glimpses are somewhat problematic. One thing we can do with them, the psychological thing, is to use them to explain away certain similar glimpses caught in adult years. Another way to understand them is to find them valid, to accept such intuitions both early and later in life as one kind of experience of reality. If we can do that, we can remember them with gratitude

. . . for those first affections
Those shadowy recollections,
Which be they what they may,
Are yet the fountain light of all our day,
Are yet a master light of all our seeing. . . .

This is another way to say what Ruth Beebe Hill also reports from the traditions of the Lakotah people, quoted in the headnote of this chapter. The glimpse of authentic togetherness given us, for example, in song, is the true and valid power of song, offering us the experience of unity with what seems to lie apart from ourselves.

Notes

INTRODUCTION

1   Text of song and critics' comments are quoted from Peter Seng, *The Vocal Songs in the Plays of Shakespeare: A Critical History* (Cambridge, Mass.: Harvard University Press, 1967), pp. 123–24. I have modified the Folio printing by including the full refrain lines where they are indicated by abbreviations after the first stanza and by using the modern forms of the letters *s* and *v*. Warburton, 1747; Capell, 1779; Steevens, 1793.

2   Ibid.

3   Ibid., p. 127, from Hotson's *The First Night of Twelfth Night* (London: Rupert Hart-Davis, 1954).

4   Ibid., pp. 125–26, from *Twelfth Night*, ed. M. Luce (London: Methuen, 1929).

5   Ibid., p. 127, from "Twelfth Night and the Morality of Indulgence," *Sewanee Review* 67 (1959): 220–38.

6   Ibid., from Catherine Ing, *Elizabethan Lyrics* (London: Chatto and Windus, 1951). The tune we are familiar with was sung and possibly composed by Joseph Vernon; he printed it in 1772, although it may be older. Cf. Seng, pp. 129, 297.

7   Auden and Chester Kallman, "Introduction" to Auden, Kallman, and Noah Greenberg, eds., *An Elizabethan Song Book* (New York: Doubleday, 1956), pp. xvi–xvii; Bronson, "Introduction" to Bronson, ed., *The Traditional Tunes of the Child Ballads*, 4 vols. (Princeton: Princeton University Press, 1959–72), 1 : ix–xi; see also his one-volume *Singing Tradition of the Child Ballads* (Princeton: Princeton University Press, 1976), pp. xxvii–xxix. On the music attainable by words alone see Kenneth Burke, "On Musicality in Verse," *The Philosophy of Literary Form* (1941; reprint ed., New York: Vintage, 1957), pp. 296–304, and Northrop Frye, "Introduction: Lexis and Melos," in Frye, ed., *Sound and Poetry* (New York: Columbia University Press, 1957), pp. ix–xxvii.

8   Lord, *The Singer of Tales* (Cambridge, Mass.: 1960; reprint ed., New York: Atheneum, 1965).

9   *Art and Illusion* (Princeton: Princeton University Press, 1960), p. 205.

10 *The Human Use of Human Beings* (1950; reprint ed., New York: Doubleday, Anchor Books, 1954), p. 21.

11   A useful comparison of song verses and poetry is made by Charles Hart-
      man, "The Criticism of Song," *Centennial Review* 19 (Spring 1975):
      96–107, especially 102–04. With the following discussion compare his
      observations that "songs tend toward repetition . . . rhetorical formula
      . . . duplication of lines . . . refrain" (p. 104).
12   Francis James Child, *The English and Scottish Popular Ballads*, 5 vols.
      (1882–98), texts 84A, 275A, 7B, 112B. There are many examples.
13   "Joe Hill," by Alfred Hayes, music by Earl Robinson, © 1938 by Leeds
      Music; "I Dreamed I Saw St. Augustine," © 1968 by Dwarf Music.
14   No. 346 in Richard L. Greene, *The Early English Carols*, 2d. ed., rev.
      and enl. (Oxford: Clarendon Press, 1977), p. 209. Cf. his introduction,
      p. clxx: "A number of carol-burdens embody expressions which served
      the Middle Ages as proverbs or bywords."
15   "You Don't Mess Around with Jim," by Jim Croce, © 1971 by Blending-
      well Music.
16   "Wedding Day in Funeralville," by John Prine, © 1975 by Sour Grapes/
      Cotillion.
17   No. 237 in William S. Baring-Gould and Ceil Baring-Gould, *The Anno-
      tated Mother Goose* (1962; reprint ed., Cleveland: Meridian, 1972), p.
      153. Cf. n. 41: "'Polly Put the Kettle On' was originally a popular coun-
      try dance and song."
18   "Back Gnawing Blues," in *The Blues Line: A Collection of Blues Lyrics*,
      comp. Eric Sackheim (New York: Grossman, 1969), p. 95; attributed to
      Ramblin' (Willard) Thomas.
19   "Hello Goodbye," by John Lennon and Paul McCartney, © 1967 by
      Northern Songs.
20   Late medieval popular song quoted by John Stevens, *Music and Poetry in
      the Early Tudor Court* (London: Methuen, 1961), p. 46, from a manu-
      script in the Hunterian Museum at Glasgow.
21   "Breakdown (A Long Way from Home)," by Kris Kristofferson, from *The
      Silver Tongued Devil and I*, Monument Records Z 30679, BMI; copyright
      information not given. C. M. Bowra, *Primitive Song* (New York: World,
      1962), pp. 83–85, notes that both rhyme and alliteration are common in
      primitive song in many languages.
22   "Simplicity and Complexity in the Elizabethan Air," *Rice University
      Studies* 51 (1965): 4. See also Doughtie, *Lyrics from English Airs, 1596–
      1622* (Cambridge, Mass.: Harvard University Press, 1970), pp. 30–41.
23   "Chicken Cordon Bleus," by Steve Goodman, Paula Ballan, and Toni
      Mandel, from Steve Goodman, *Somebody Else's Troubles*, Buddha Rec-
      ords BDS 5121, © 1972.
24   No. 46 in *Secular Lyrics of the XIVth and XVth Centuries*, ed. Rossell
      Hope Robbins (Oxford: Clarendon Press, 1952), pp. 41–42.
25   Lehmann, *Eighteen Song Cycles: Studies in their Interpretation* (London:
      Cassell, 1971), p. 6.
26   Bowra, *Primitive Song*, p. 32.
27   Child no. 79.

28   Child no. 58; "The Ballad of Hollis Brown," © 1963 by M. Witmark & Sons. See *Writings and Drawings by Bob Dylan* (New York: Knopf, 1973), p. 86.

29   Copyright 1965 by M. Witmark & Sons; Dylan, *Writings and Drawings*, p. 199.

30   *Man the Musician*, trans. Norbert Gutterman, Bollingen Series 44.2 (Princeton: Princeton University Press, 1973), p. 51.

·31   Ibid., p. 42.

32   Ibid., pp. 24–25, 26–27; italic in the original—the closest of several agreements between Dr. Zuckerkandl's analysis and my own, which was first done before I encountered his work.

33   Ibid., p. 29.

34   Ibid., p. 41.

35   "Elizabethan Air," pp. 4–6. Doughtie quotes Raynor, "Words for Music," *Monthly Musical Record* 88 (1958): 179–80.

36   Doughtie, "Elizabethan Air," p. 3; Bowra, *Primitive Song*, p. 68.

CHAPTER 1

1   British Museum MS. Harley 978, f. 11ᵇ. Both this song and the Latin "Perspice christicola" that is interlined with it are performed on the recording *Medieval English Lyrics*, Argo Record Company ZRG 5443, London, 1965.

      The instructions read: "This round can be sung by four. It should not be performed, however, by fewer than three, or at least by two, besides those who sing the burden. But this is how it should be sung. While the others are silent, one begins with those who carry the burden. And when he comes to the first note after the cross, another enters, and so with the others. But each one halts again at the indicated rests, and not elsewhere, for the duration of one long note"; and for the two forms of the burden: "One repeats this as long as necessary, pausing at the end," and "the other sings this pausing in the middle and not at the end, but immediately returning to the beginning" (my translation).

2   Arthur K. Moore, *Secular Lyrics in Middle English* (Lexington: University of Kentucky Press, 1951), p. 51. See the strictures of Robert D. Stevick, "Criticism of Middle English Lyrics," *Modern Philology* 64 (1966): 103–17.

3   Stephen Manning, "Sumer is icumen in," *Explicator* 18 (1959): item 2.

4   Edmund Reiss, *The Art of the Middle English Lyric* (Athens, Ga.: University of Georgia Press, 1972), p. 9. A date of about 1310 was proposed by Manfred Bukofzer, "'Sumer is icumen in'—a Revision," *University of California Publications in Music*, vol. 2, no. 2, pp. 79ff.; the older date is upheld by B. Schofield, "Provenance and Date of 'Sumer is Icumen in,'" *Music Review* 9 (1948): 81–86.

5   "Of Ballads, Songs, and Snatches," in his *Ballad as Song* (Berkeley and Los Angeles: University of California Press, 1969), p. 292.

6   A & M Records 1335. It appeared on the *Billboard* top pop 100 list for
    fourteen weeks, reaching a ranking of number six. Joel Whitburn, *Top
    Pop Records, 1955–1972* (Menomonee Falls, Wis.: Record Research,
    1973), p. 229.
7   Reiss, *Art of the Middle English Lyric*, pp. 9, 11.
8   Ibid., p. 10.
9   Ibid., p. 11.
10 Chambers and Sidgwick, *Early English Lyrics, Amorous, Divine, Moral
    & Trivial* (1907; reprint ed. Sidgwick and Jackson, 1947), p. 4; Quiller-
    Couch, *Oxford Book of English Verse, 1250–1918* (1900; New Edition,
    Oxford: Clarendon Press, 1939), p. 1.
11 Reiss, *Art of the Middle English Lyric*, p. 12.
12 "Literate Orality of Popular Culture," in *Rhetoric, Romance, and Tech-
    nology* (Ithaca: Cornell University Press, 1971), p. 290.
13 Sanders, "Polyphony and Secular Monophony: Ninth Century—c. 1300,"
    in *Music from the Middle Ages to the Renaissance*, ed. F. W. Sternfeld,
    the Praeger History of Western Music, vol. 1 (New York: Praeger, 1973),
    pp. 120, 126.
14 Ibid., p. 115.
15 "The Motet and Allied Forms," in Hughes, ed., *Early Medieval Music up
    to 1300*, the New Oxford History of Music, vol. 2 (1954; rev. ed., Lon-
    don: Oxford University Press, 1955, pp. 354, 373.
16 "Wired for Sound," in *The Barbarian Within* (New York: Macmillan,
    1962), p. 222.
17 Quoted by Harold Gleason, in *Music in the Middle Ages and Renais-
    sance*, Music Literature Outline, ser. 1 (Rochester: Levis Music Stores,
    1967), p. 53. The passage is translated by C. Baumbach from J. Wolf,
    "Die Musiklehre des Johannes de Grocheo," *Sammelbände der interna-
    tionalen Musikwissenschaft* 1 (1894): 65.
18 See Sanders, pp. 89–90, 98, 125–26.

CHAPTER 2

1   Text from Greene, *A Selection of English Carols* (Oxford: Clarendon Press
    1962), pp. 92–93. See the "Introduction," pp. 33–34, and the notes,
    pp. 209–10; cf. his *Early English Carols*, p. 82 (carol no. 136A), "In-
    troduction," pp. cxxii–cxxvii, and notes.
2   Cf. Greene, *Early English Carols*, p. clvii: Christmas was "a time when
    ribald songs were much in evidence." He quotes a Latin indictment of
    the practice of singing such songs from Thomas Gascoigne in the fif-
    teenth century.
3   Cf. Gilbert Murray, *The Classical Tradition in Poetry* (New York: Vintage,
    1957), p. 39: "In most of the dances, if not all, the dancer ceased to be
    himself. . . . The hierophant in the mysteries regularly became identi-
    fied with the god, the leader of the Bacchic dance became Bacchos."

4   Greene, *Early English Carols*, pp. cxxiv–cxxvi, collects references.
5   For an example in stained glass see Bernard Rackham, *The Ancient Glass of Canterbury Cathedral* (London: Humphries, 1949), monochrome plate no. 22a. Nesta de Robeck, *The Christmas Crib* (London: Catholic Book Club, 1937), remarks that the Franciscans took crèche ritual "into France, England, Spain, and Germany" sometime after 1223 (p. 62). Play quoted from Joseph Quincy Adams, *Chief Pre-Shakespearean Dramas* (Cambridge, Mass.: Riverside, 1924), p. 25, from a French source, but the play "existed in England (there are allusions to it in the twelfth-century Statutes of Lichfield)."
6   E. Stredder, *Notes and Queries*, 8th ser., vol. 9, p. 4.

CHAPTER 3

1   The text and the account of its recovery are given by Frank Sidgwick in *Notes and Queries*, 10th ser., 4 (1905): 84–85.
2   "The Ballad of *The Bitter Withy*," *PMLA* 23 (1908): 141–67; chapbook text quoted on p. 160.
3   For a full statement of the view that such characteristics as incremental repetition prove a folk origin, see Francis B. Gummere, *The Beginnings of Poetry* (New York, 1901). Louise Pound argued that such forms are more the product of oral transmission than of conditions of origin: *Poetic Origins and the Ballad* (New York, 1921), chap. 4. A full history of the controversy is given in D. K. Wilgus, *Anglo-American Folksong Scholarship Since 1898* (New Brunswick, N.J.: Rutgers University Press, 1959). David Buchan (see note 5) and others have used the Parry-Lord conception of oral composition to analyze what is formulaic in the ballads, although some scholars reject such analysis, and also Buchan's diagrammatic analysis of ballad structures that is referred to below in the text.
4   Cf. "Knight and Shepherd's Daughter" (Child no. 110B), a distant analogue of the *Wife of Bath's Tale*, where casual rape is made good by marriage, and then class fantasy is indulged by a sudden revelation:

> *But when they came unto the place*
>   *Where marriage rites were done*
> *She proved her self a duke's daughter*
>   *And he but a squire's son.*

Such a reversal presumably cheers even more of the ballad's audience, men and women alike, than the women's victory of the marriage itself.
5   *The Ballad and the Folk* (London: Routledge & Kegan Paul, 1972), pp. 53, 94–95.
6   *The Origin of Consciousness in the Breakdown of the Bicameral Mind* (Boston: Houghton Mifflin, 1976), p. 365. Jaynes, in whose work I first met this evidence, employs it in arguing a remarkable thesis about the

nature and history of consciousness. One conclusion of his study is that early poetry-song originated in activity of the right brain independent of activity or awareness in the left, to which it was delivered by a hallucinated voice.

7   "Hemispheric lateralization of singing after intra-carotid sodium amylobarbitone," *Journal of Neurology, Neurosurgery and Psychiatry* 37 (1974): 732–33.

8   Ibid., p. 733.

9   Bogen, "The Other Side of the Brain II: An Appositional Mind," *Bulletin of the Los Angeles Neurological Societies* 34 (1969): 150, 158.

10   J. Levy-Agresti and R. W. Sperry, quoted by Bogen, "Other Side of the Brain II," p. 149.

11   "Laterality Effects in Audition," in *Interhemispheric Relations and Cerebral Dominance*, ed. Vernon Mountcastle (Baltimore: Johns Hopkins University Press, 1962), pp. 177–79.

12   Wasserman, *The Finer Tone: Keats' Major Poems* (Baltimore: Johns Hopkins University Press, 1953), pp. 68 and passim; 11–62; Bate, *John Keats* (Cambridge, Mass.: Harvard University Press, 1963), pp. 417, 416.

13   R. G. Peterson, "Critical Calculations: Measure and Symmetry in Literature," *PMLA* 91 (1976): 367–75, surveys recent critical work on annular and other patterns in literature, including Catullus, Shakespeare, Pope, and Fielding. He concludes that such patterns are real, although not consciously recognized by writers, readers, or critics before the twentieth century. The present discussion offers a way to understand what he calls "the trouble . . . that . . . there is no evidence that writers who are supposed to have used such patterns knew about them" (p. 368).

CHAPTER 4

1   Text from *The Works of Thomas Campion*, ed. Walter R. Davis (New York: Norton, 1970), pp. 22–23, where the music is also printed. The song is recorded on Archive Productions (D.G.G.) 14501 APM, ARC 3004, "The High Renaissance: Series M, the Elizabethan Age." On *A Booke of Ayres*, see Ralph W. Berringer, "Thomas Campion's Share in *A Booke of Ayres*," *PMLA* 58 (1943): 938–48; for history, see Edward Doughtie's introduction to his *Lyrics from English Airs, 1596–1622*. The body of Doughtie's book is a full edition of the airs of this period other than Campion's.

2   For the history of the courtly tradition and its relation to song, see John Stevens, *Music and Poetry in the Early Tudor Court* (London: Methuen, 1961).

3   Berringer, "Thomas Campion's Share in *A Booke of Ayres*," p. 941.

4   Irwin, "Thomas Campion and the Musical Emblem," *Studies in English Literature* 10 (1970): 122.

5   Davis, *Works of Campion*, p. 22 n.
6   Davis, "Melodic and Poetic Structure: the Examples of Campion and Dowland," *Criticism* 4 (1962): 94.
7   David I. Masson, "Vowel and Consonant Patterns in Poetry," in *Essays on the Language of Literature*, ed. Seymour Chatman and Samuel R. Levin (Boston: Houghton Mifflin, 1967), p. 3.
8   Booth, *Shakespeare's Sonnets* (New Haven: Yale University Press, 1977), p. xi.
9   Cited by Dell Hymes, "Phonological Aspects of Style: Some English Sonnets," in Chatman and Levin, *Essays on the Language of Literature*, from Sapir's essay, "A Study of Phonetic Symbolism."
10 Partridge, *Shakespeare's Bawdy: A Literary and Psychological Essay and a Comprehensive Glossary* (New York: Dutton, 1955), pp. 89–90 on *come*, p. 95 on *country*; Hymes, "Phonological Aspects of Style," p. 38.
11 Hollander, *Vision and Resonance: Two Senses of Poetic Form* (New York: Oxford University Press, 1975), p. 78, in his chapter, "The Case of Campion."
12 *Childhood and Society*, 2d ed. (New York: Norton, 1963), p. 250; cf. also p. 80.
13 Phrases from a tale in *African Myths and Tales*, ed. Susan Feldman (New York: Dell, 1963); Stith Thompson, ed., *Motif-Index of Folk Literature*, rev. ed., 6 vols. (Bloomington: Indiana University Press, 1966), vol. 1.
14 Irwin, "Thomas Campion and the Musical Emblem," p. 135.
15 "The Metaphysical Poets," in *T. S. Eliot: Selected Essays* (New York: Harcourt Brace, 1950), pp. 248, 242–43.
16 "Words and Music," in *Elizabethan Poetry*, Stratford-upon-Avon Studies, no. 2 (New York: St. Martin's Press, 1960), pp. 148–49.
17 *Music and Poetry in the Early Tudor Court*, p. 28.
18 *An Essay on Shakespeare's Sonnets* (New Haven: Yale University Press, 1969), pp. 36, 51; Booth, *Shakespeare's Sonnets*, p. xiii.
19 Fish, *Self-Consuming Artifacts* (Berkeley and Los Angeles: Univ. of California Press, 1972), p. 386.
20 Booth, *Shakespeare's Sonnets*, pp. x, xiv.
21 Fish, *Self-Consuming Artifacts*, p. 389 (Fish's emphasis).

CHAPTER 5

1   Text and woodcut are taken from Hyder E. Rollins, ed., *A Pepysian Garland: Black-Letter Broadside Ballads of the Years 1595–1639* (1922; reprint ed., Cambridge, Mass.: Harvard University Press, 1971), pp. 438–42. On Parker see Rollins, "Martin Parker, Ballad-Monger," *Modern Philology* 16 (1919): 113–38. The tune "Bragandary" is lost.
2   "The Black-Letter Broadside Ballad," *PMLA* 34 (1919): 258, 259.
3   Sixteen ballads by Parker are printed in Rollins, *A Pepysian Garland*. One of his pieces, "A True Tale of Robin Hood," was included in the

Child collection (no. 154), because of its apparent relationship to older lost versions of the Robin Hood legend. On the history of the street ballads generally see *The Common Muse: An Anthology of Popular British Ballad Poetry, 15th–20th Century*, ed. Vivian de Sola Pinto and Allan Edwin Rodway (1957; reprint ed., London: Penguin, 1965), pp. 32–48; Albert B. Friedman, *The Ballad Revival: Studies in the Influence of Popular on Sophisticated Poetry* (Chicago: University of Chicago Press, 1961), chap. 2; and Leslie Shepard, *The Broadside Ballad: A Study in Origin and Meaning* (1962; reprint ed., Hatboro, Pa.: Legacy Books, 1978).

4   See Peter Dronke, *The Medieval Lyric* (New York: Harper, 1969).

5   Rollins, *Pepysian Garland*, no. 57, p. 331.

6   Ibid., n. 58, p. 334.

7   Ibid., p. xi; Pinto, *Common Muse*, p. 48.

8   *The Bagford Ballads*, ed. Joseph Woodfall Ebsworth, 2 vols. (Hertford, 1876–80; reprint ed., New York: AMS, 1968), 1:250; the number of the ballad is Bagford Collection II, 80.

9   On the way in which tunes became popular and on the origins of the practice of singing printed ballads, see John Ward, "Music for *A Handefull of Pleasant delites*," *JAMS* 10 (1957): 151–80.

10 *The British Broadside Ballad and Its Music* (New Brunswick, N.J.: Rutgers University Press, 1966), p. xix.

11 Ibid., p. 225.

12 Ibid., p. 570.

CHAPTER 6

1   *Boswell's Life of Johnson*, ed. G. B. Hill, rev. L. F. Powell, 6 vols. (Oxford: Clarendon Press, 1934–50), 2:368.

2   *Some Versions of Pastoral* (Norfolk, Conn.: New Directions, n.d.), p. 195.

3   *Dunciad* (1729), bk. iii, line 326n.

4   *The Oxford Companion to Music*, 9th ed. (London: Oxford University Press, 1965), p. 972, s.v. "Song." See also his entries under "Ballad Opera" and "*The Beggar's Opera*." For convincing argument on Gay and Pepusch, see Bertrand H. Bronson, "The Beggar's Opera," in *Facets of the Enlightenment* (Berkeley and Los Angeles: University of California Press, 1968), pp. 76–77.

5   Claude M. Simpson, *The British Broadside Ballad and Its Music*, p. xiv; Phyllis Hartnoll, ed., *Shakespeare In Music* (1964; reprint ed., New York: St. Martin's Press, 1966), pp. ix, 9.

6   Bronson, "The Beggar's Opera," p. 63.

7   "*The Beggar's Opera* in Its Own Time," in *Twentieth Century Interpretations of the Beggar's Opera*, ed. Noble (Englewood Cliffs, N.J.: Prentice-Hall, 1975), p. 12.

8   Bronson, "The Beggar's Opera," pp. 63–64.

9   "The Black-Letter Broadside Ballad," *PMLA* 34 (1919): 287–88.

10   *Broadside Ballad and Its Music*, pp. 103–04. American appearances of the ballad include a condensation into a three-stanza lament. G. Malcolm Laws, Jr., *American Balladry from British Broadsides* (Philadelphia: American Folklore Society, 1957), pp. 290–91. Cole Porter parodied the song in his "Two Little Babes in the Woods," for the musical *Paris* in 1928.

11   "Gay" in *Lives of the English Poets by Samuel Johnson, LL.D.*, ed. G. B. Hill, 3 vols. (Oxford: Clarendon Press, 1905), 2:277, n. 6.

12   "Towards Defining an Age of Sensibility," in *Fables of Identity: Studies in Poetic Mythology* (New York: Harcourt, Brace and World, 1963), p. 135.

CHAPTER 7

1   "Letter to Marcellinus," in *Athanasius*, trans. Robert C. Gregg (New York: Paulist Press, 1980), pars. 28, 11, 29, 31.

2   See John Julian, ed., *A Dictionary of Hymnology*, 2 vols. (1907; reprint ed., New York: Dover, 1957), under "Methodist Hymnody" (G. J. Stevenson), "Wesley Family" (J. H. Overton and Julian), and "Love divine, all loves excelling" (Julian). The text is taken from Frank Baker, *Representative Verse of Charles Wesley* (New York: Abingdon, 1962), pp. 94–96, and represents the first published form, in *Hymns for those that Seek, and those that Have Redemption in the blood of Jesus Christ*, 1747.

3   Julian, *Dictionary of Hymnology*, pp. 1259–60; J. Ernest Rattenbury, *The Evangelical Doctrines of Charles Wesley's Hymns* (London: Epworth, 1941), p. 20; Frank Baker, *Charles Wesley's Verse: An Introduction* (London: Epworth, 1964), pp. 5–6; Katherine Smith Diehl, *Hymns and Hymn Tunes—An Index* (New York: Scarecrow, 1966), pp. xx, 176, 535–39.

4   Baker, *Charles Wesley's Verse*, p. 34, quoting Moulton, *Proceedings of the Wesley Historical Society*, 1:26–27, and Rattenbury, *Evangelical Doctrines*, pp. 47–52. Henry Bett, *Hymns of Methodism* (London: Epworth, 1945), pp. 72, 134, 154, says some of the references found by Moulton are "rather faint" echoes but that fourteen are unmistakable quotations. Curiously, the title line of that hymn is from Milton, as that of "Love Divine" is from Dryden.

5   Bett, *Hymns of Methodism*, p. 29. Cf. Donald Davie, "The Classicism of Charles Wesley," in *Purity of Diction in English Verse* (1952: reprint ed., New York: Schocken, 1967), pp. 73ff.

6   Robert Guy McCutcheon, *Our Hymnody, A Manual of the Methodist Hymnal* (New York: Methodist Book Concern, 1937), p. 388 (cf. Rattenbury, *Evangelical Doctrines*, p. 37); Alfred Burton Haas, "Charles Wesley," in *Papers of the Hymn Society*, ed. James Rawlings Sydnor (New York, 1957), 22:18.

7   Baker, *Charles Wesley's Verse*, p. 55; Bernard Manning, *Hymns of Wesley and Watts* (London: Epworth, 1942), p. 21.

8   George H. Findlay, *Christ's Standard Bearer* (London: Epworth, 1956), p. 26. A comma was added after *heaven* in 1780, making the reading as a prayer stronger. Baker, *Representative Verse of Charles Wesley*, p. 94.

9   See the account of John Wesley's expurgation and the indignant objection of R. Newton Flew, *Hymns of Charles Wesley: A Study of their Structure* (London: Epworth, 1953), pp. 53–54; see also George John Stevenson, *The Methodist Hymn Book, Illustrated with Biography, History, Incident, and Anecdote* (London, 1883), pp. 266–67.

10   Jeremiah Bascom Reeves, *The Hymn as Literature* (New York: Century, 1924), p. 176.

11   "Waller," in/Hill, *Lives of the English Poets by Samuel Johnson*, 1:291.

12   Baker, *Charles Wesley's Verse*, p. 17.

13   *Hymns and Sacred Poems, in Two Volumes* (Bristol, 1756), p. 177.

14   Baker, *Representative Verse of Charles Wesley*, p. 96.

CHAPTER 8

1   Stan Hugill, *Shanties from the Seven Seas* (New York: Dutton, 1961), pp. 207–08, from the singing of Paddy Delaney (Blackballer) and Bill Fuller. I have respelled *wuz* and dropped quotation marks from the transcription. Other versions are given on pp. 203–14. See also William Main Doerflinger, *Shantymen and Shantyboys* (New York: Macmillan, 1951), pp. 17–22.

2   *The Medieval Lyric* (London: Hutchinson and Co., 1968), p. 15: Chrysostom, *Patrologia Graeca* 55. 156–57.

3   Hugill, *Shanties from the Seven Seas*, pp. 42 (distribution), 20–23 (origins of name), 2–20 (early history); Roger D. Abrahams, *Deep the Water, Shallow the Shore: Three Essays on Shantying in the West Indies* (Austin: University of Texas Press, 1974). Cf. Doerflinger, *Shantymen*, pp. 91ff., and Hugill, *Shanties and Sailors' Songs* (New York: Praeger, 1969), pp. 1–66.

4   Hugill, *Shanties from the Seven Seas*, p. 26; *Shanties and Sailors' Songs*, pp. 83–85, with a helpful diagram on p. 84.

5   Bruce Jackson, *Wake Up Dead Man: Afro-American Worksongs from Texas Prisons* (Cambridge, Mass.: Harvard University Press, 1972), p. 18; Harold Courlander, *Negro Folk Music, U.S.A.* (New York: Columbia University Press, 1965), p. 91; Frederick Pease Harlow, *Chanteying Aboard American Ships* (Barre, Mass.: Barre Gazette, 1962), p. 2.

6   Jackson, *Wake Up Dead Man*, pp. 19, 26.

7   *The Origin of Consciousness in the Breakdown of the Bicameral Mind* (Boston: Houghton Mifflin, 1976), p. 427.

8   *Essay Concerning Human Understanding*, ed. Peter H. Nidditch (Oxford: Clarendon Press, 1975), p. 182 (bk. 2, chap. 14, par. 4).

9   Jackson, *Wake Up Dead Man*, p. 18.

10   Hugill, *Shanties from the Seven Seas*, pp. 200–01.

11   Ibid., pp. 107, 108, 211, 219, 307, 372, 374.

12   Ibid., pp. 300, 335, 469.

13   Ibid., p. 401.

14   Ibid., p. 208.

15   Ibid., p. 200; Abrahams, *Deep the Water, Shallow the Shore*, p. 63; Doerflinger, *Shantymen*, p. 17.

16   Hugill, *Shanties from the Seven Seas*, pp. 291, 290, 72, 251. Gordon Bok sings and prints "Gimme" to start a chorus line in "Where Am I to Go" but credits the song to Hugill, who prints "To me" (*Seven Seas*, p. 167). Since Bok reports learning other songs in service under sail, his change has some authority. See *A Tune for November*, Folk-Legacy Records FSI-40, 1970, enclosed pamphlet of the same title, and liner notes.

17   Hugill, *Shanties from the Seven Seas*, pp. 66, 72, 82, 87, 90, 97.

18   Ibid., p. 134.

19   Ibid., p. 286.

20   Jackson, *Wake Up Dead Man*, p. 30.

CHAPTER 9

1   Text, including somewhat erratic punctuation, as reprinted in *Favorite Songs of the Nineties: Complete Original Sheet Music for 89 Songs*, ed. Robert A. Fremont (New York: Dover, 1973), pp. 2–5. Sales estimates are from David Ewen, *Popular American Composers* (New York: H. W. Wilson, 1962), pp. 84–85 (five million), and from Ian Whitcomb, *After the Ball: Pop Music from Rag to Rock* (New York: Simon and Schuster, 1972), pp. 3–4 (ten million within twenty years); and see under Foster in Ewen, *Popular American Composers*, p. 64.

2   David Ewen, *All the Years of American Popular Music* (Englewood Cliffs, N.J.: Prentice-Hall, 1977), p. 154.

3   See, for example, Anne Wilson, *Traditional Romance and Tale: How Stories Mean* (Ipswich, England: D. S. Brewer, 1976), pp. vii, 30, 50.

4   Charles K. Harris, *After the Ball: Forty Years of Melody* (New York: Frank-Maurice, 1926), pp. 117, 132, 143, 171, 183.

5   James D. Hart, *The Popular Book: A History of America's Literary Taste* (Berkeley and Los Angeles: University of California Press, 1961), p. 98.

6   *Reveries of a Bachelor; or, A Book of the Heart*, New Edition (New York, 1873), pp. 93, 303, 237.

7   Ibid., pp. 20–21, 97.

8   Ibid., p. 261.

9   Harris, *After the Ball: Forty Years of Melody*, pp. 341–47, 102.

10   Ibid., pp. 14–15, 27, 53, 105, 108, 139, 158.

11   Ibid., pp. 226–28.

12   Ibid., pp. 94–95.

13   "American Victorianism As a Culture," *American Quarterly* 27 (1975): 522. On competitiveness see also Burton Bledstein, *The Culture of Professionalism: the Middle Class and the Development of Higher Education in America* (New York: Norton, 1976); on the legacy of Victorian values for contemporary culture see Philip Slater, *The Pursuit of Loneliness: American Culture at the Breaking Point*, rev. ed. (Boston: Beacon Press, 1976). I am indebted to Professor R. Gordon Kelly for introducing me to these books.

14   *Shorter Bartlett's Familiar Quotations* (reprint ed., New York: Permabooks, 1953), seven entries. The heading does not appear in all editions.

CHAPTER 10

1   Hit records for Jimmy Dean in 1961, Jim Croce in 1973, Barry Sadler in 1966, Gordon Lightfoot in 1977. See Stephen Nugent and Charlie Gillett, eds., *Rock Almanac: Top Twenty American and British Singles and Albums of the '50's, '60's, and '70's* (New York: Doubleday, Anchor Books, 1978). The tone of strut is, for example, James Brown's line, "I'm a man and a half."

2   The first broadcast advertisement was in 1923: Frank Presbrey, *The History and Development of Advertising* (Garden City: Doubleday, Doran & Co., 1929), p. 529. On early commercials see Herman S. Hettinger, *A Decade of Radio Advertising* (1933; reprint ed., New York: Arno, 1971), pp. 261, 264. On the Wheaties jingle see Miles David and Kenneth Costa, "Since 1895, radio finds its niche in media world," in *How It Was In Advertising* (Chicago: Crain, 1976), pp. 97–99. (They cite a "counterclaim for a Tasty Yeast jingle that is said to have been broadcast in 1925," p. 97.)

3   Text and piano transcription of the Wheaties and Pepsi-Cola jingles are available in *Great Songs of Madison Avenue*, ed. Peter and Craig Norback (New York: Quadrangle, 1976), pp. 72–73, 146–47. See E. S. Turner, *The Shocking History of Advertising!* (New York: Dutton, 1953), p. 321; *New York Times*, Dec. 19, 1943, sec. 2, p. 7, col. 1, and Oct. 29, 1944, sec. 6, pp. 26–27; Roger D. Abrahams, ed., *Jump-Rope Rhymes: A Dictionary* (Austin: University of Texas Press, 1969), p. 159; Mary and Herbert Knapp, *One Potato, Two Potato . . .* (New York: Norton, 1976), p. 163: "Pepsi-Cola hits the spot, / Ties your belly in a knot, / Tastes like vinegar, looks like ink, / Pepsi-Cola is a stinky drink."

4   See *New York Times*, July 3, 1960, sec. 3, p. 10, col. 1; Oct. 31, 1976, sec. 3, p. 31.

5   Oct. 31, 1976, sec. 3, p. 3, col. 1.

6   Recorded by Gary Glitter, Slade, Suzi Quatro, Donny Osmond, and 10 cc. See Nugent and Gillett, *Rock Almanac*, p. 366.

7   *English in Advertising: A Linguistic Study of Advertising in Great Britain* (London: Longmans, 1966), p. 193.

CHAPTER 11

1 Watt, *The Rise of the Novel: Studies in Defoe, Richardson, and Fielding* (Berkeley and Los Angeles: University of California Press, 1965), especially chap. 1; on *Robinson Crusoe*, see chap. 3.

2 *Richmond* (Va.) *Times-Dispatch*, May 14, 1979, p. A-3, from an Associated Press dispatch.

3 Norris McWhirter, et al., *1979 Guinness Book of World Records* (New York: Sterling, 1978), p. 247.

4 See C. A. Schicke, *Revolution in Sound: a Biography of the Recording Industry* (Boston: Little, Brown, 1974), pp. 81–86.

5 Pleasants, *The Great American Popular Singers* (New York: Simon and Schuster, 1974), p. 142.

6 Ibid., p. 129.

7 Marguerite Haymes, quoted in ibid., p. 134.

8 Pleasants, *Great American Popular Singers*, pp. 16, 35.

9 Ibid., p. 26.

10 Recorded the same spring as "White Christmas," Crosby's "Silent Night" sold seven million records that year and many more in subsequent seasons. Joseph Murrells, in his *Book of Golden Discs* (London: Barrie and Jenkins, 1974), pp. 41, 407, cites unconfirmed reports that its sales have approached those of "White Christmas." "Silent Night" ranked first and "White Christmas" second among Americans' favorite Christmas songs in a 1950 Gallup Poll.

11 See David Foulkes, "How Do Hypnagogic Dreams Differ from REM Dreams?" in *The New World of Dreams*, ed. Ralph L. Woods and Herbert B. Greenhouse (New York: Macmillan, 1974), p. 323.

12 See Stuart Albert and William Jones, "The Temporal Transition from Being Together to Being Alone: the Significance and Structure of Children's Bedtime Stories," in *The Personal Experience of Time*, ed. Bernard S. Gorman and Alden E. Wessman (New York: Plenum Press, 1977), pp. 109–32.

13 Murrells, *Book of Golden Discs*. p. 407.

14 See the brief history and extensive bibliography in my chapter "Popular Music" in *Handbook of American Popular Culture*, ed. M. Thomas Inge (Westport, Conn.: Greenwood Press, 1978), pp. 171–93.

15 "Desolation Row," *Writings and Drawings by Bob Dylan*, p. 195; "Banana Republics," by Steve Goodman, Steve Burgh, and Jim Rothermel, from Goodman's album *Words We Can Dance To*.

CONCLUSION

1 See Linda Ferrill Annis, *The Child Before Birth* (Ithaca: Cornell University Press, 1978), pp. 52–57; J. C. Grimwade et al., "Human fetal heart rate change and movement in response to sound and vibration," *Ameri-*

220

NOTES TO PAGES 199–203

can Journal of Obstetrics and Gynecology 109 (1 Jan. 1971): 86–90; in the same issue, David Walker et al., "Intrauterine noise: A component of the fetal environment," pp. 91–95; John C. Eccles, "Creation of the Self," *Bulletin of the Menninger Clinic* 43 (Jan. 1979): 12.

2   "The role of the heartbeat in the relation between mother and infant," *Scientific American* 228 (May 1973); 25–29.

3   Hugill, *Shanties and Sailors' Songs*, p. 93 ("Hanging Johnny"); South African lullaby cited by Theresa C. Brakeley in *Funk and Wagnalls Standard Dictionary of Folklore*, ed. Maria Leach (New York, 1972), s.v. *lullaby*.

4   Brakeley (see n. 3, above).

5   On the australopithecines, see Frank B. Livingstone, with responses from other scholars, *Current Anthropology* 14 (1973): 25–26; the speculation about song before and leading to speech seems to have been offered first by Otto Jesperson, *Language, Its Nature, Development and Origin* (London: Allen and Unwin, 1922); C. M. Bowra, *Primitive Song*, pp. 57–58.

6   Holland, *The Dynamics of Literary Response* (New York: Oxford University Press, 1968), pp. 64–65.

7   Ibid., pp. 66, 78.

8   *Endymion* bk. I, lines 777–801; see also his letter to his publisher John Taylor, 30 January 1818.

Index

221